First published in the United Kingdom in 2011 by
Collins & Brown
10 Southcombe Street
London
W14 0RA

An imprint of Anova Books Company Ltd

Design and text copyright © Collins & Brown 2011
Programme and format copyright © Avalon
  Entertainment Ltd 2010

All rights reserved. No part of this publication may be reproduced, stored in a retrieval system, or transmitted in any form or by any means electronic, mechanical, photocopying, recording or otherwise, without the prior written permission of the copyright owner. The patterns contained in this book and the items created from them are for personal use only. Commercial use of either the patterns or items made from them is strictly prohibited.

ISBN 978-1-84340-625-9

A CIP catalogue for this book is available from the British Library.

10 9 8 7 6 5 4 3 2 1

Reproduction by Rival Colour Ltd, UK
Printed by Toppan Leefung Printing Limited, China

This book can be ordered direct from the publisher at www.anovabooks.com

CONTENTS

FOREWORD	**7**
SO YOU WANT TO LEARN TO KNIT?	**8**
THE K FACTOR: **THE ACTION FROM ROUND 1**	**16**
THE KNITTED CHARACTER	**18**
SO YOU WANT TO LEARN TO CROCHET?	**20**
KNITTED SIMON COWELL	**24**
KNITTED SIMON COWELL'S MEANEST K FACTOR MOMENTS	**29**
KNITTED CHERYL COLE	**30**
KNITTED ROLANDO OFF POPSTAR TO OPERASTAR	**34**
THE K FACTOR: **THE ACTION FROM ROUND 2**	**38**
PETER THE DUCK	**40**

PETER THE DUCK'S BEST K FACTOR MOMENTS	42
WINSTON STIMSON	44
NINJA CLOWN	48
THE K FACTOR: THE ACTION FROM ROUND 3	54
PHILNUT	56
GARY	60
KNITTED SPIDER-MAN	64
THE K FACTOR: THE ACTION FROM ROUND 4	68
THE REAL KNITTED HARRY HILL	70
HARRY HILL MEERKAT	74
KNITTED HARRY HILLS	78
KNITTED HARRY HILL WEEK	83
THE K FACTOR: THE ACTION FROM ROUND 5	84
BRYAN AND CAROLINE	86
THE ACTION FROM THE NOT LIVE FINAL: K FACTOR ON ICE	92
CROCHET CONFESSION	94
AND THE WINNER IS...	95
PUBLISHER'S ACKNOWLEDGEMENTS	96
TECHNIQUES AND ABBREVIATIONS	96

FOREWORD

When I launched The K Factor and asked the public to submit their knitted contestants I expected at most about twenty. In the end we received over 10,000! As I digged deeper I discovered a huge sister and brotherhood of dedicated knitters, a new wave of people not content with knitting cardigans and scarves but who strove to create, from wool, images of our great cultural icons – like Spider-Man, Hitler and Jesus and his Disciples. I had no idea that knitting was in such rude health in this country!

I think we all remember where we were when Peter the Duck lifted the coveted K Factor trophy, but who amongst us can remember the detail? The way Winston Stimson's eyes filled with tears as he told us of his tragic back-story? The jaunty angle of Philnut's Y-Fronts? And the look of disappointment from Bryan as his new bride Caroline ditched him for her chance at the top of the knitted showbiz pile?

Well now you can have it all back – for the first time in one place you have the blueprint to run your own K Factor. What better way to mark TV's most important knit-based talent competition than to knit the contestants and judges yourself?

This book is to the K Factor what The Bayeux Tapestry is to the Battle of Hastings.

Now that's enough from me.

Get knitting!

SO YOU WANT TO LEARN TO KNIT?

KNITTING BASICS
Here's all you need to know to help you create your very own K Factor characters.

WORKING FROM A PATTERN
Before starting any pattern, always read it through. This will give you an idea of how the design is structured and the techniques that are involved. Each pattern includes the following basic elements:

Materials
This will include the amount of yarn, the sizes of needles and any buttons or felt that you might need. The yarn amounts specified are based on average requirements and are therefore approximate.

The needle size is only a suggested needle size. Tension (gauge), how tightly or loosely a knitter knits, can vary quite dramatically. This is because of the way that the needles and the yarn are held. For the characters in this book a firm fabric is required and a suggested tension (gauge) is given at the beginning of each pattern. To check what your tension is knit a tension (gauge) swatch.

Tension swatch instructions
Use the same needles, yarn and stitch pattern as those that will be used for the main work and knit a sample at least 12.5cm (5in) square. Smooth out the finished piece on a flat surface, but do not stretch it.

To check the stitch tension, place a ruler horizontally on the sample, measure 10cm (4in) across and mark with a pin at each end. Count the number of stitches between the pins. To check the row tension, place a ruler vertically on the sample, measure 10cm (4in) and mark with pins. Count the number of rows between the pins. If the number of stitches and rows is greater than specified in the pattern, make a new swatch using larger needles; if it is less, make a new swatch using smaller needles.

Project instructions
Knitting instructions are normally given in an abbreviated form. The most commonly used abbreviations and those used in this book are listed on page 96.

Before starting to knit your K Factor character, read the instructions carefully to understand the abbreviations used, how the design is structured and in which order each piece is worked. However, there may be some parts of the pattern that only become clear when you are knitting them, so do not assume that you are being slow or that the pattern is wrong.

Asterisks or brackets are used to indicate the repetition of a sequence of stitches. For example: * k3, P1; rep from * to end. This means, knit three stitches, then purl one stitch, then repeat this sequence to the end of the row. It could also be written: [k3, P1] to end.

The phrase 'work even' means continue without increasing or decreasing the number of stitches and keeping the established pattern correct.

HARRY'S HINT Don't be a knit. When you put your knitting aside, always mark where you are on the pattern – it's better to be safe than sorry!

Making up
The Making Up section in each project will tell you how to join the knitted pieces together. Always follow the recommended sequence.

A BASIC CAST ON
Casting on is the term used for making a row of stitches to be used as a foundation for your knitting.

MAKING A SLIP KNOT
A slip knot is the basis of all casting-on techniques and is therefore the starting point for almost everything you do in knitting.

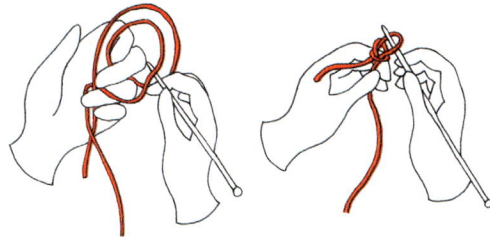

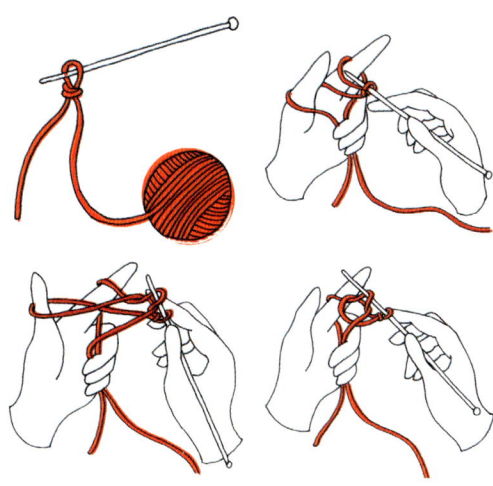

1. Wind the yarn around two fingers twice, as shown. Insert a knitting needle through the first (front) strand and under the second (back) one.
2. Using the needle, pull the back strand through the front one to form a loop. Holding the loose ends of the yarn with your left hand, pull the needle upwards, tightening the knot.

1. Place the slip knot on the needle, leaving a long tail, and hold the needle in your right hand.
2. *Wind the loose end of the yarn around your thumb from front to back. Place the ball end of the yarn over your left forefinger.
3. Insert the point of the needle under the loop on your thumb. With your right index finger, take the ball end of the yarn over the point of the needle.
4. Pull a loop through to form the first stitch. Remove your left thumb from the yarn. Pull the loose end to secure the stitch. Repeat from * until the required number of stitches has been cast on.

HARRY'S HINT No matter how excited you are about knitting your very own K Factor character, and how annoying it seems to have to spend time knitting a tension swatch before you start, it really is worth taking the time to do it!

9

LACE CAST ON

The lace cast on is an open and stretchy cast on. Do not mistake it for the cable cast on.

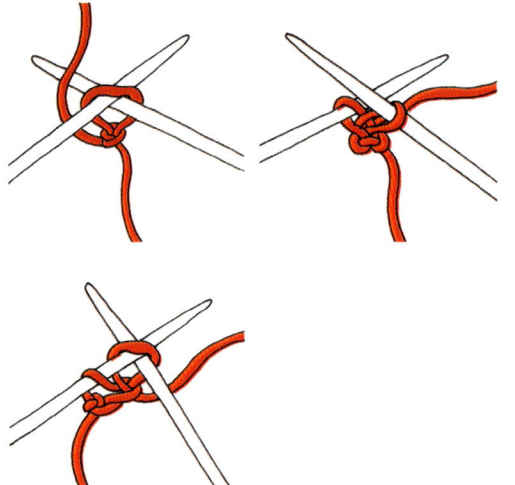

1. Leaving a short tail of 10cm, place the slip knot on the needle and hold the needle in your left hand. *Insert the right-hand needle from left to right through the front of the slip knot or last stitch on the left-hand needle.
2. Wrap the yarn from left to right over the point of the right-hand needle.
3. Draw the yarn through the stitch and gently pull the new stitch loop until it is long enough to reach the tip of the left-hand needle. Place the stitch loop onto the left-hand needle, remove the right-hand needle and pull the yarn so that the stitch loop fits snugly around the left-hand needle.
4. Repeat from * until the required number of stitches has been cast on.

THE BASIC STITCHES

The knit and purl stitches form the basis of all knitted fabrics. The knit stitch is the easiest to learn. Once you have mastered this, you can move on to the purl stitch.

Knit stitch (K)

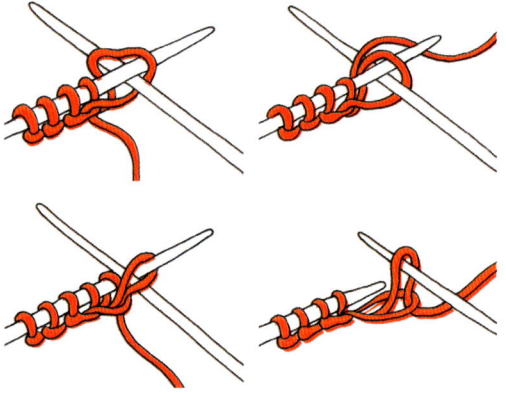

1. Hold the needle with the cast-on stitches in your left hand. Insert the right-hand needle from left to right through the front of the first stitch on the left-hand needle.
2. Wrap the yarn from left to right over the point of the right-hand needle.
3. Draw the yarn through the stitch, thus forming a new stitch on the right-hand needle.
4. Slip the original stitch off the left-hand needle, keeping the new stitch on the right-hand needle. To knit a row, repeat steps 1 to 4 until all the stitches have been transferred from the left-hand needle to the right-hand needle.

HARRY'S HINT Use a pair of needles that is one size larger to cast on so that the cast-on row isn't tight when knitting the first row.

HARRY'S HINT Try using a ring pull from a drinks can as an effective (and cheap!) marker for your knitting.

Purl stitch (P)

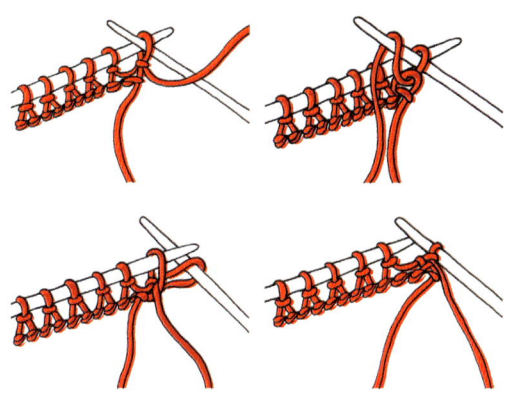

1. Hold the needle with the stitches in your left hand, with the loose yarn at the front of the work. Insert the right-hand needle from right to left into the front of the first stitch on the left-hand needle.
2. Wrap the yarn from right to left, up and over the point of the right-hand needle.
3. Draw the yarn through the stitch, thus forming a new stitch on the right-hand needle.
4. Slip the original stitch off the left-hand needle, keeping the new stitch on the right-hand needle. To purl a row, repeat steps 1–4 until all the stitches have been transferred from the left-hand needle to the right-hand needle.

Knit through the back loop (Ktbl)

Work as for a knit stitch but insert the right-hand needle from left to right through the back of the first stitch on the left-hand needle.

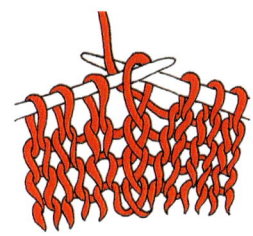

Purl through the back loop (Ptbl)

Work as a purl stitch but insert the right-hand needle from left to right through the back of the first stitch on the left-hand needle.

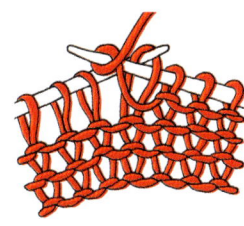

Slip stitch (sl)

Following the stitch pattern set, insert the right-hand needle into the first stitch on the left-hand needle as if to knit or purl. Transfer it onto the right-hand needle without wrapping the yarn around the right-hand needle to make a new stitch.

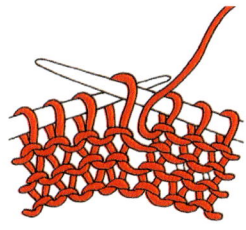

SHAPING

This is achieved by increasing or decreasing the number of stitches you are working.

Increasing

The simplest method of increasing one stitch is to create two stitches out of stitch. Work a stitch into the front of the stitch to be increased into; then, before slipping it off the needle, place the right-hand needle behind the left-hand one and work again into the back of it (inc). Slip the original stitch off the left-hand needle.

Decreasing (K2tog, K2togtbl, P2tog P2togtbl)

The simplest method of decreasing one stitch is to work two stitches together.

To knit two stitches together (k2tog), insert the right-hand needle from left to right through the front of the second stitch, then first stitch nearest the tip of the left-hand needle and knit them together as one stitch.

To knit two together through the back loops (k2togtbl), insert the right-hand needle from right to left through the back of the first, then second stitch nearest the tip of the left-hand needle and knit them together as one stitch.

To purl two stitches together (p2tog), insert the right-hand needle from right to left through the front of the first then second stitch from the tip of the left-hand needle, then purl them together as one stitch.

To purl two together through the back loops (p2togtbl), insert the right-hand needle from left to right through the back of the second, then first stitch nearest the tip of the needle and purl them together as one stitch.

Making a stitch (M1)

Another form of increasing involves working into the strand between two stitches.

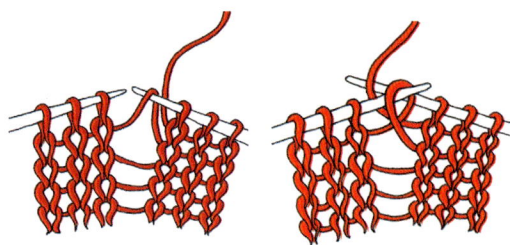

1. Insert the right-hand needle from front to back under the horizontal strand that runs between the stitches on the right- and left-hand needles.
2. Insert the left-hand needle under the strand from front to back, twisting it as shown, to prevent a hole from forming, and knit (or purl) through the back of the loop. Slip the new stitch off the left-hand needle.

Making a yarn forward (yfwd)

A yarn forward is a loop of yarn placed over the right-hand needle which is worked on following rows like any other stitch and creates a hole in the knitted fabric.

Work to the position of the yarn forward and bring the yarn forward (towards you) between the tips of the needles. Then, take the yarn backwards (away from you) over the right-hand needle and knit the next stitch.

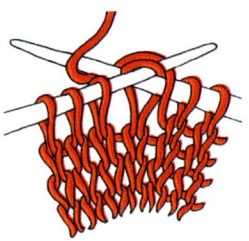

SPECIAL STITCHES

Loop stitch is a variation of double crochet and is usually worked on wrong-side rows because the loops form at the back of the fabric.

Loop (Fur) stitch

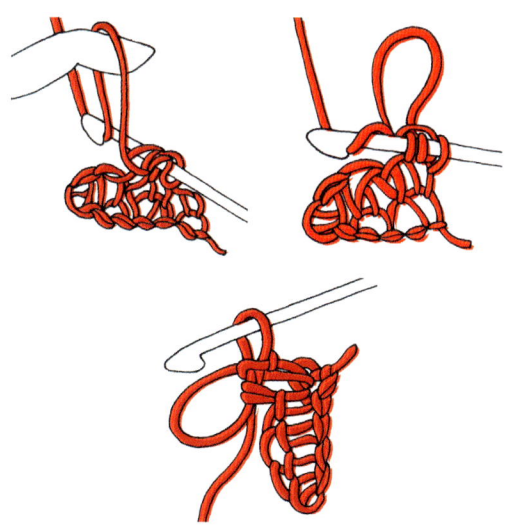

1. Insert hook into the stitch below. Using a free finger, pull up the yarn to form a loop. Pick up both strands of the loop and draw through.
2. Wrap the supply yarn over the hook.
3. Draw the yarn through all three loops.

NOTE: When each loop is cut afterwards, the texture of the fabric resembles fur or hair.

CASTING OFF

This is the most commonly used method of securing stitches once you have finished a piece of knitting. The cast-off edge should have the same 'give' or elasticity as the fabric.

Knitwise

Knit two stitches. * Using the point of the left-hand needle, lift the first stitch on the right-hand needle over the second, then drop it off the needle. Knit the next stitch and repeat from * until all stitches have been worked off the left-hand needle and only one stitch remains on the right-hand needle. Cut the yarn, leaving enough to sew in the end, thread the end through the stitch, then slip it off the needle. Draw the yarn up firmly to fasten off.

Purlwise

Purl two stitches. * Using the point of the left-hand needle, lift the first stitch on the right-hand needle over the second and drop it off the needle. Purl the next stitch and repeat from * until all the stitches have been worked off the left-hand needle and only one stitch remains on the right-hand needle. Secure the last stitch as described in casting off knitwise.

HARRY'S HINT Cast off in the same stitch you used for the main fabric unless the pattern says otherwise.

SEWING BASICS

FINISHING TECHNIQUES

You may have finished knitting but there is one crucial step still to come, the sewing up of the seams. It is tempting to start this as soon as you cast off the last stitch but a word of caution, make sure that your have good light and plenty of time to complete the task. It would be a shame to spoil your K Factor character because you rushed this final stage.

Mattress stitch (side edges)

This stitch makes an almost invisible seam on the knit side of stocking stitch. Thread a tapestry needle with yarn and position the pieces side by side, right sides facing.

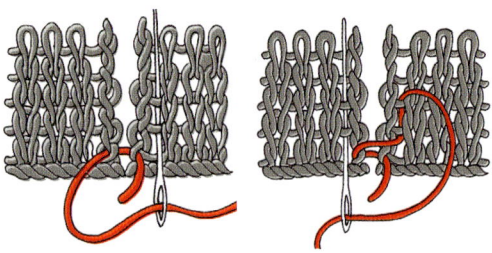

1. Working from the bottom of the seam to the top, come up from back to front at the base of the seam, to the left of the first stitch in from the edge, on the left-hand side and leave a 10cm tail of yarn. Take the needle to across to the right-hand piece, to the right of the first stitch, pass the needle under the first two of the horizontal bars that divide the columns of stitches above the cast on.

2. Take the needle to across to the left-hand piece, insert the needle down where it last emerged on the left-hand edge, pass the needle under two of the horizontal bars that divide the columns of stitches. Take the needle to across to the right-hand piece, insert the needle down through the fabric where it last emerged on the right-hand edge, pass the needle under the first two of the horizontal bars that divide the columns of stitches above the cast on. Repeat step 2 until the seam has been closed.

Mattress stitch (top and bottom edges)

Thread a tapestry needle with yarn and position the pieces top and bottom, right sides facing outermost. Working left to right, come up from back to front through the centre of first stitch on the right

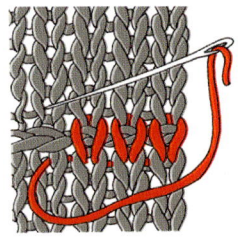

edge of the seam and leave a 10cm tail of yarn. Take the needle to across to the top piece, pass the needle under the two loops of the stitch above, then go down again, through the fabric, where the needle emerged on the lower piece. Repeat with the next stitch to the left.

Inserting stuffing

As with all soft toys, how you stuff your doll will directly affect the finished appearance. It is important to stuff firmly, but without stretching the knitting out of place. Always stuff down the extremities, such as the legs and arms, first and mould into shape as you go along. The amount of stuffing needed for each doll depends on the knitting tension and individual taste.

French knots

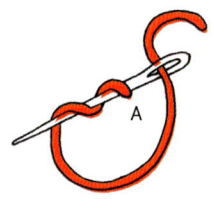 

1. Come up at A and wrap the thread around the needle once in an anti-clockwise direction. Wrap the thread around the needle a second time in the same direction, keeping the needle away from the fabric.
2. Push the wraps together and slide to the end of the needle. Go down close to the start point, pulling the thread through to form a knot.

Swiss darning or duplicate stitch

This embroidery stitch duplicates the appearance of a knit stitch by following the passage of the yarn through the fabric.

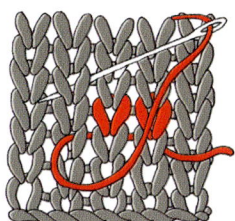 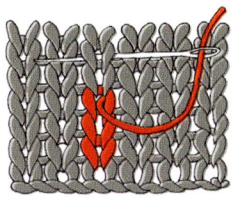

Come up at the base of the stitch, A, then pass the needle under the two loops of the stitch above, and then go down again at A. Repeat with the next stitch to the either the left or above of the last embroidered stitch.

Running stitch

Work a series of short straight stitches to create a dashed line of stitches. Come up at A, go down at B and then come up at C. Do not pull the thread through the fabric. Go down at D and come up at E. Pull the thread through gently, so that the fabric does not pucker. Repeat as necessary, keeping the stitches even.

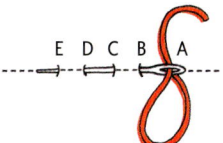

Backstitch

Work a series of short straight stitches to create a solid line of stitches. Working from right to left, come up at A, go down at B and then come up at C. Pull the thread through. Go down again at B to make a backstitch, then come up at D, ready for the next stitch, and continue.

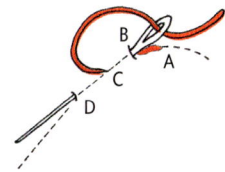

Satin stitch

Work a series of short straight stitches, parallel to each other, to create a pad of stitches.

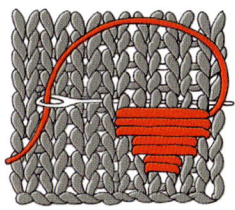

15

THE K FACTOR
THE ACTION FROM ROUND 1

With over 2,000 entries, competition for knitted characters throughout the land to win places in the K Factor Not Live Final has been extremely fierce.

"THE STANDARD HAS BEEN REALLY HIGH."

"SHE THOUGHT I WAS A GOOD EXAMPLE OF AN OLD-FASHIONED TOY FOR GEORGE'S PROJECT ABOUT WORLD WAR II."

First up is Winston Stimson from Bedford, knitted by Linda Stimson for her grandson, George.

WINSTON'S LAUNDRY NIGHTMARE

What the judges don't know about Winston is that he has a tragic back-story. When he was young, his mum once put him into the washing machine by mistake.

"I NEARLY DROWNED."

His heart-wrenching tale moves the judges, and he is put through to the next round of the competition.

Ninja Clown is the next auditionee. Knitted Simon doesn't like his hat, but after pleading with the judges, Ninja Clown goes through.

"PLEASE, SIMON, I WON'T LET YOU DOWN."

Peter the Duck, from Croydon, is not so lucky – Knitted Cheryl turns him down.

"YOU HAVEN'T GOT ANY WINGS, PET. SORRY, IT'S A 'NO'."

Next to go on is Philnut from Norwich. The judges are confused by his choice of outfit, as Philnut has come onstage in only his underpants. Knitted Simon recognises his potential, nonetheless.

"YOU COULD GO A LONG WAY IN THIS COMPETITION."

I'M GARY. I WAS KNITTED BY MADDIE, WHO IS 14 AND LIVES IN LINCOLN. A LOT OF PEOPLE THINK I LOOK LIKE TOBY YOUNG.

Gary is the next contestant to make it through.

Christine from Yorkshire is up next, sporting a knitted balaclava.

IT MEANS A LOT - IT'S MY LIFE!

The Knitted Character is impressed, calling her knitting "stylish and cool". Christine is through.

It's been a long day, and the last knitted act to meet the judges is married couple Amos and Ruth. After some disagreement about exactly how old they are, they finally agree that they're 82 years old.

WE'RE 82.

WE'RE 82.

The judges put them through to the next round.

17

THE KNITTED CHARACTER

JUDGE

The king of the knitted world, The Knitted Character is a TV Burp regular. On The K Factor, his positive, constructive criticism ("it's practical, and looks really cool") made him a popular judge with the contestants on the show. However, in a dramatic twist during the Not Live Final week, he dropped a bombshell by revealing to Harry Hill that he isn't actually knitted at all – he's crocheted!

FACT FILE

Name: *The Knitted Character.*
Interesting fact: *He likes jelly.*
K Factor high: *Working with Knitted Cheryl Cole.*
K Factor low: *His crochet confession.*

MATERIALS
Cream Patons Diploma Gold DK, approx 120m/50g ball (55% wool, 45% acrylic)
    1 ball in Cream 6142
    1 ball in Pink 6219

Oddment of black for face

Crochet hooks: 3.5mm and 2.25mm

SO YOU WANT TO LEARN TO CROCHET?

CROCHET BASICS

The basics of crochet are very similar to that of knitting. Read through the pattern carefully, noting the materials suggestions and any unfamiliar abbreviations, then, work a tension swatch about 12.5cm (5in) square using the suggested yarn and hook size.

To check the stitch tension, pin out an area 10cm (4in) square and count the number of rows and stitches between the pins. If the number of stitches and rows is greater than specified in the pattern, make a new swatch using a larger hook; if it is less, make a new swatch using a smaller hook. Now you are ready to crochet your K Factor character.

Double crochet (dc)

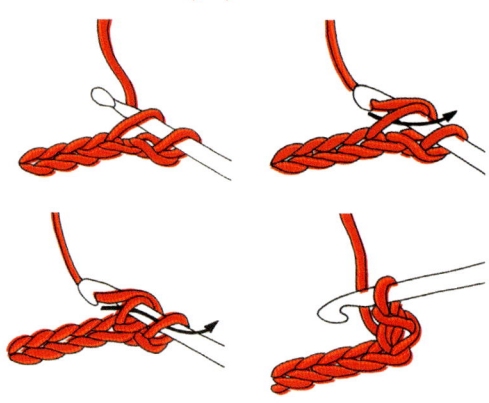

1. To work the first row, make a foundation chain to the required length, adding 1 chain to allow for turning. Insert your hook into the second chain below the hook.
2. *Insert the hook into the chain or stitch indicated, wrap the yarn around the hook from back to front, draw the yarn through the crochet fabric – there are two loops on the crochet hook.
3. Wrap the yarn around the hook from back to front, draw the yarn through both loops on the hook.
4. One complete double crochet stitch has been made. To continue, repeat from *.

Chain (ch)

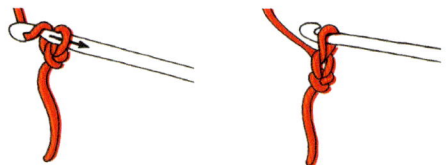

1. Hold the yarn in the left hand, using your preferred method, and at the same time keep a good tension on the tail end of the yarn. *Wrap the yarn around the hook from back to front, draw the yarn towards the slip knot or loop, rotate the hook so it is facing downwards and ease the yarn through the slip knot or the loop on the hook.
2. Rotate the hook so that the hook is left facing up and the new stitch is resting on the hook. Continue to work from * to create more chain stitches. You will need to reposition the tensioning fingers of your left hand every couple of stitches to ensure a good tension on the yarn.

Treble crochet (tr)

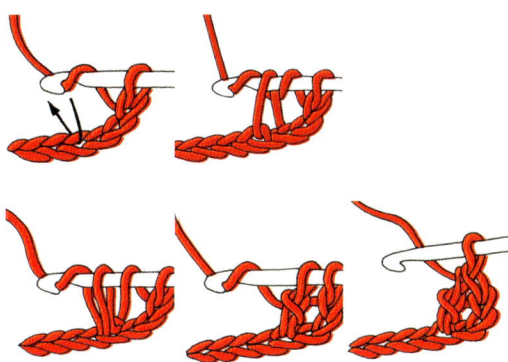

1. To work the first row, make a foundation chain to the required length, adding 3 chain to allow for turning. *Wrap the yarn around the hook (from back to front) once. Insert the hook into the fourth chain below the hook.
2. Insert the hook into the chain or stitch indicated, wrap the yarn around the hook from back to front, draw the yarn through the crochet fabric – there are three loops on the crochet hook.
3. Wrap the yarn around the hook from back to front, draw the yarn through two loops of the hook – there are two loops on the crochet hook.
4. Wrap the yarn around the hook from back to front, draw the yarn through both loops on the hook.
5. One complete treble crochet stitch has been made. However, because the turning chain, in this case, is counted, two treble crochet stitches have been created. To continue, repeat from *.

Joining in a new yarn

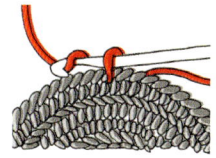

To crochet stripes, fasten off and join in yarn as required – this produces a neater finish.

For working in rows, fasten off the previous yarn, then, with the side that is about to be worked facing, insert hook into the top of the last stitch, wrap the new yarn around the hook and draw the yarn through the crochet fabric – there is one loop on the crochet hook. Make the required number of chain to work the chosen stitch then continue to work in new yarn as required.

Slip stitch (sl st)

Insert the hook into the stitch or place indicated, wrap the yarn around the hook from back to front, draw the yarn through both the crochet fabric and the loop on the crochet hook.

A slip stitch at the end of a round is used to join the last stitch to the first stitch. Insert the hook under both top loops of the first stitch of the round, wrap the yarn around the hook from back to front, draw the yarn through both the top loops and the loop on the crochet hook.

Decreasing

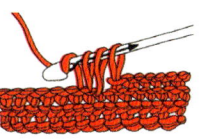

Insert the hook into the next stitch, wrap the yarn around the hook and draw the yarn through the crochet fabric – there are two loops on the crochet hook. Insert the hook into the following stitch, wrap the yarn around the hook and draw the yarn again through the crochet fabric – there are three loops on the crochet hook. Wrap the yarn around the hook and draw through all the loops on the hook.

TENSION

20sts and 20 rows over 10cm.

BODY

Using cream yarn and 3.5mm hook make 20ch + 1ch.

Row 1: 1dc into 2nd ch from hook, 1dc into next and every ch to end, turn.

Row 2: 1ch, 1dc into next 4dc, 2dc into next dc, 1dc into next 10dc, 2dc into next dc, 1dc into next 4dc, turn. (22sts)

Break off cream, join in pink.

Row 3: 1ch, 1dc into next 5dc, 2dc into next dc, 1dc into next 10dc, 2dc into next dc, 1dc into next 5dc, turn. (24 sts)

Break off pink and join in cream. Work the next 17 rows in dc in following stripe sequence:

Rows 4–7: Cream.
Row 8: Pink.
Rows 9–12: Cream.
Row 13: Pink.
Rows 14–17: Cream.
Row 18: Pink.
Rows 19–20: Cream.

Row 21: 1ch, 1dc into 1st st, dc2tog over next 2sts, * 1dc into next 2sts, dc2tog over next 2sts, rep from * to last st, 1dc into last st. (18sts)

Row 22: 1ch, 1dc into 1st st, * dc2tog over next 2sts, rep from * to last st, 1dc into last st, turn. (10sts)

Row 23: 1ch, 1dc into each st to end. Repeat last row twice more.

Break off yarn. Sew in all loose ends. Sew up back seam. Insert ample stuffing from bottom. Sew up bottom seam. Insert a little more stuffing at neck to make sure it's going to hold the head – do not sew up.

HEAD

Using cream yarn and 3.5mm hook make 2ch.

Rnd 1: Work 8dc into 2nd ch from hook, sl st into top of 2nd ch to complete round. (8sts)

Rnd 2: 1ch, 1dc into each dc to end, sl st into top of 1ch at beg of round.

Rnd 3: 1ch, work 2dc through back loop into next and every dc to end, sl st into top of 1ch at beg of round. (16sts)

Rnd 4: 1ch, 1dc into 1st dc, 2dc into next dc, *1dc into next dc, 2dc into next dc, rep from * to end, sl st into top of 1ch at beg of round. (24sts)

Rnd 5: 1ch, 1dc into each of the 1st 2dc, 2dc in next dc,* 1dc into each of the next 2dc, 2dc into next dc, rep from * to end, sl st into top of 1ch at beg of round. (32sts)

Rnd 6: 1ch, 1dc into each of the 1st 3dc, 2dc in next dc,* 1dc into each of the next 3dc, 2dc into next dc, rep from * to end, sl st into top of 1ch at beg of round. (40sts)

Rnds 7–9: 1ch, 1dc into 1st and every dc to end, sl st into top of 1ch at beg of round.

Rnd 10: 1ch, 1dc into 1st 3dc, work dc2tog over next 2dc,*1dc into next 3dc, dc2tog over next 2dc, rep from * to end, sl st into top of 1ch at beg of round. (32sts)

Rnd 11: 1ch, 1dc into 1st and every dc to end, sl st into top of 1ch at beg of round.

Rnd 12: 1ch, 1dc into 1st 2dc, work dc2tog over next 2dc, *1dc into next 2dc, dc2tog over next 2dc, rep from * to end, sl st into top of 1ch at beg of round. (24sts)

Rnd 13: as rnd 11.

Rnd 14: 1ch, 1dc into 1st dc, work dc2tog over next 2dc, *1dc into next dc, dc2tog over next 2dc, rep from * to end, sl st into top of 1ch at beg of round. (16sts)

Rnd 15: as rnd 11.

Rnd 16: 1ch, * work dc2tog over next 2dc, rep from * to end, sl st into top of 1ch at beg of round. (8sts)

Break off yarn. Leave enough length to sew up back seam.

Insert stuffing into head, making sure to stuff the nose.

Sew up back opening.

Take a length of cream yarn and thread an embroidery needle. Do not secure or tie knot. Insert needle where rounds have been joined at Round 3 and weave in and out of stitches around neck. Pull tight and tie a double knot. Sew in loose ends. Sew head to body making sure that the place where the rounds were joined is at the bottom.

LEGS (MAKE 2)
Using cream yarn and 3.5mm hook make 4ch + 1ch.
Row 1: Work 2dc into 2nd ch from hook, then work 2dc into each ch to end, turn. (8sts)
Row 2: 1ch, 1dc into each dc to end, turn.
Row 3: 1ch, work 2dc into each of the 1st 2dc, work 1dc into next 4dc, then work 2dc into each of the last 2dc, turn. (12sts)
Row 4: 1ch, 1dc into each dc to end.
Row 5: as row 4.
Row 6: 1ch, 2dc into each of the 1st 2dc, work 1dc into next 8dc, then work 2dc into last 2dc, turn. (16sts)
Row 7: 1ch, 1dc into each dc to end.
Row 8: as row 7.
Row 9: 1ch, (dc2tog over next 2sts) 3 times, 1dc into next 4dc, (dc2tog over next 2sts) 3 times, turn. (10sts)
Row 10: 1ch, 1dc into each dc to end.
Break off cream yarn, join in pink. Work the next 16 rows as row 10 in following stripe sequence.
Row 11: Pink.
Rows 12–15: Cream.
Row 16: Pink.
Rows 17–20: Cream.
Row 21: Pink.
Rows 22–25: Cream.
Break off yarn.
Sew in all loose ends. Sew up back seam and sole of foot.
Insert ample stuffing from top down, then sew up top seam.

ARMS (MAKE 2)
Using cream yarn and 3.5mm hook make 5ch + 1ch.
Row 1: Work 2dc into 2nd ch from hook, then work 2dc into each ch to end, turn. (10sts)
Rows 2: 1ch, 1dc into each dc to end, turn.
Work the next 19 rows as row 2 in following stripe sequence.
Row 3: Cream.
Row 4: Pink.
Rows 5–8: Cream.
Row 9: Pink.
Rows 10–13: Cream.
Row 14: Pink.
Rows 15–18: Cream.
Row 19: Pink.
Rows 20–21: Cream.
Row 22: 1ch, (dc2tog over next 2sts) twice, 1dc into next 2dc, (dc2tog over next 2sts) twice, turn. (6sts)
Break off yarn. Sew in all loose ends. Sew up back seam.
Insert ample stuffing from top down. Sew up top seam.
Using picture as a guide, attach arms and legs to body, making sure that both feet are pointing to the front.

EARS (MAKE 2)
Using cream yarn and 2.25mm hook work 3ch + 1ch.
Row 1: 1dc into 2nd ch from hook, 1dc into each ch to end, turn.
Row 2: 1ch, 1dc into each dc to end, turn.
Row 3: 1ch, 1dc into 1st dc, 2dc into next dc, 1dc into last dc. (4sts)
Rows 4–6: 1ch, 1dc into each dc to end.
Row 7: 1ch, work (dc2tog over 2sts) twice. (2sts)
Row 8: 1ch, dc2tog over 2sts.
Break off yarn and pull through loop on hook. Sew in loose end at top of ear, leave end at base chain for sewing onto head. Using picture as guide, pin then stitch ears onto head.

FACE
Using picture as guide, embroider face. Use black DK yarn split into two threads.
Nose: satin stitch.
Mouth: back stitch.
Eyes: satin stitch.

SCARF
Using pink yarn and 3.5mm hook work 3ch + 3ch.
Row 1: Work 1tr into 4th ch from hook then each ch to end. (3sts)
Row 2: 3ch, miss 3ch, work 1tr into next and each tr to end.
Repeat last row a further 23 times or until required length achieved.
Break off yarn, sew in loose ends.
Tie scarf round neck in a bow.

KNITTED SIMON COWELL
JUDGE

Arguably one of the most powerful knitted characters on television, Knitted Simon Cowell is both feared and revered in equal measure. Famed for his brutal honesty and straight-talking, underneath those high-waisted knitted trousers beats a heart of gold. In The K Factor, we saw him beheaded by a jilted groom, facing the wrath of Peter the Duck's supporters, dealing with a Knitted Fathers for Justice protester, and saving Peter the Duck's life after his attempted suicide, declaring: "I love you, Peter – you're through."

MATERIALS
Patons Fab DK, approx 274m/100g ball (100% acrylic)
    1 ball in Black 2311
    1 ball in Red 2323
    1 ball in White 2306
Sirdar Bonus DK, approx 280m/100g ball (100% acrylic)
    1 ball in Flesh 963
Pair of 3.75mm needles

One D-ring, 32mm
One black felt square

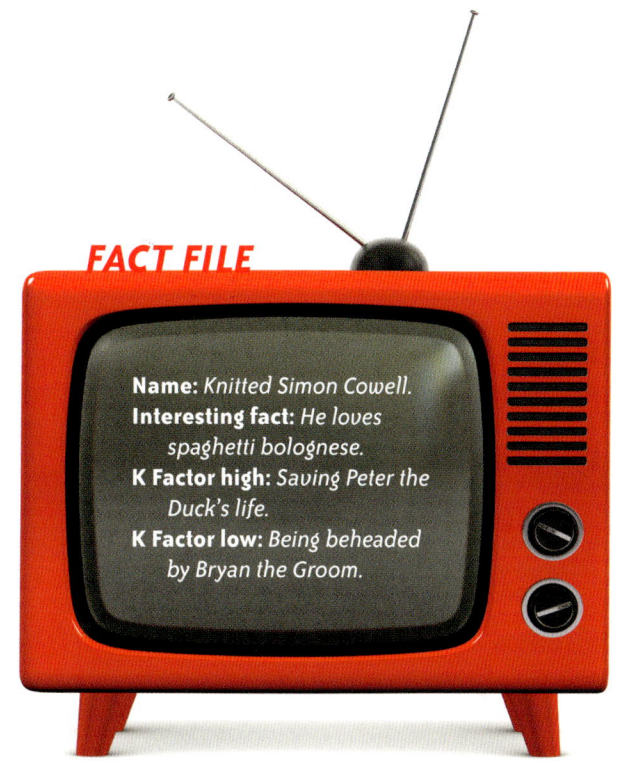

FACT FILE

Name: *Knitted Simon Cowell.*
Interesting fact: *He loves spaghetti bolognese.*
K Factor high: *Saving Peter the Duck's life.*
K Factor low: *Being beheaded by Bryan the Groom.*

TENSION
23 stitches and 32 rows over 10cm stocking stitch.

BODY
Using 3.75mm needles and black yarn, cast on 40 sts.
Row 1 (WS): Purl to end.
Row 2 (RS): K9, m1, k2, m1, k18, m1, k2, m1, k9. (44 sts)
Row 3: Purl to end.
Row 4: K10, m1, k2, m1, k20, m1, k2, m1, k10. (48 sts)
Row 5: Purl to end.
Row 6: K11, m1, k2, m1, k22, m1, k2, m1, k11. (52 sts)
Row 7: Purl to end.
Rows 8–29: Stocking stitch.
Row 30: K10, K2tog, k2, k2togtbl, k20, k2tog, k2, k2togtbl, k10. (48 sts)
Row 31: Purl to end.
Rows 32-41: Stocking stitch.
Row 42: K9, k2tog, k2, k2togtbl, k18, k2tog, k2, k2togtbl, k9. (44 sts)
Row 43: Purl to end.
Rows 44–45: Stocking stitch.
Row 46: K8, k2tog, k2, k2togtbl, k16, k2tog, k2, k2togtbl, k8. (40 sts)
Row 47: Purl to end.
Break off black and change to flesh.
Row 48: K7, k2tog, k2, k2togtbl, k14, k2tog, k2, k2togtbl, k7. (36 sts)
Row 49: Purl to end.
Row 50: K6, k2tog, k2, k2togtbl, k12, k2tog, k2, k2togtbl, k6. (32 sts)
Row 51: Purl to end.

HEAD
Row 52: K2, m1, * k3, m1, rep from * to last 3 sts, k3. (42 sts)
Row 53: Purl to end.
Row 54: K3, m1, * k4, m1, rep from * to last 3 sts, K3. (52 sts)
Row 55: Purl to end.
Row 56: K4, m1, * k5, m1, rep from * to last 3 sts, K3. (62 sts)
Row 57: Purl to end.
Row 58: Knit.
Row 59: Purl.
Repeat the last 2 rows a further 9 times.
Row 78: * K4, k2tog, rep from * to last 2 sts, k2. (52 sts)
Row 79: Purl.
Row 80: * K3, k2tog, rep from * to last 2 sts, k2. (42 sts)
Row 81: Purl.
Row 82: * K2, k2tog, rep from * to last 2 sts, k2. (32 sts)
Row 83: Purl.
Row 84: * K1, k2tog, rep from * to last 2 sts, k2. (22 sts)
Row 85: Purl.
Row 86: K1,* k2tog, rep from * to last st, k1. (12 sts)
Row 87: Purl.
Break off yarn, leaving a good length. Draw through remaining sts on needle and pull tight. Sew up back seam of head and body.
Insert ample stuffing, using picture as guide to get the correct shape.
Sew up bottom seam.
Take a length of flesh-coloured yarn and thread an embroidery needle. Do not secure or tie knot. Insert needle at back seam approx 4 rows from black row and weave in and out of stitches around neck.
Pull tight and tie a double knot.
Sew in loose ends.

BELT
Cut strip of black felt fabric long enough to fit around body (approx 3cm wide), thread the strip through a D-ring to make a belt and stitch in place.

LEGS (MAKE 2)

Using 3.75mm needles and black yarn, cast on 16 sts.
Work in stocking stitch for approx 30 rows.
Cast off.
Sew up side and bottom seam; insert stuffing and sew up top seam.

ARMS (MAKE 2)

Worked from top down.
Using 3.75mm needles and black yarn, cast on 12 sts.
Row 1: Knit.
Row 2: Purl.
Row 3: K1, m1, k3, m1, k4, m1, k3, m1, k1. (16 sts)
Starting with a purl row, work a further 5 rows stocking stitch.
Row 9: K1, m1, k4, m1, k6, m1, k4, m1, k1. (20 sts)
Starting with a purl row and ending with a knit row, work a further 8 rows stocking stitch.
Row 18: Knit.
Break off black and join in flesh.
Work a further 2 rows in stocking stitch.
Row 22: K1, k2tog, k3, (k2tog, k1) 3 times, k2, k2tog, k1. (15 sts)
Row 23: Purl.
Row 24: K1, k2tog, k2, (k2tog, k1) twice, k1, k2tog, k1. (11 sts)
Starting with a purl row, work a further 21 rows stocking stitch.
Break off yarn – leave a good length, thread through sts on needle and pull tight.
Secure yarn and sew up side seam.
Insert stuffing, then sew up top seam.
Attach arms and legs to body – use picture as guide and shaping marks on body to position arms.

HAIR

Worked from back neck up to crown, with stitches cast on for front hair line.
Using 3.75mm needles and black yarn, cast on 19 sts.
Row 1: Knit.
Row 2: K1, * L1, k1, rep from * to end.
Row 3: K1, m1, knit to last st, m1, k1. (21 sts)
Repeat last 2 rows 3 more times, then row 2 once more. (27 sts)
Row 11: Knit to end.
Row 12: K2, * L1, k1 rep from * to the last st, k1.
Row 13: Knit.
Row 14: K1, * L1, k1, rep from * to end.
Row 15: As row 3. (29 sts)

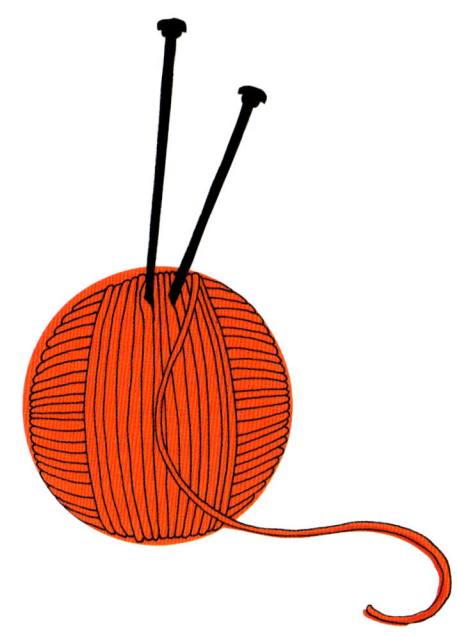

Row 16: As row 12.
Row 17: As row 3.
Row 18: K1, * L1, k1, rep from * to end, turn and cast on 17 sts.
Row 19: Knit to end. (48 sts)
Row 20: K2, * L1, k1, rep from * to end.
Start decreasing for top of head.
Row 21: K7, (K2tog) twice, * k8, (k2tog) twice, rep from * to last st, k1. (40 sts)
Row 22: K1, * L1, k1, rep from * to last st, K1.
Row 23: K5, (K2tog) twice, * k6, (k2tog) twice, rep from * to last st, k1. (32 sts)
Row 24: K1, * L1, k1, rep from * to last st k1.
Row 25: K3, (k2tog) twice, * k4, (k2tog) twice, rep from * to last st, k1. (24 sts)
Row 26: K1, * L1, k1, rep from * to last 2 sts, k2.
Row 27: K1, (K2tog) twice, * k2, (k2tog) twice, rep from * to last st, k1. (16 sts)
Row 28: K2, * L1, k1, rep from * to end.
Row 29: k1, L1, rep from * to end.
Break off yarn and thread through sts on needle; pull tight and secure. Sew up side seam.
Pin the hair to head, with cast-on edge (19 sts) at back and cast-on edge (17 sts) at front.
Sew hair to head with black yarn, using picture as guide. Leave back hair line free to insert stuffing.
Insert stuffing to make head into a square shape; once you are happy with head shape, sew up back hair line.

FACE

Using picture as guide, embroider face.
Eyes: White and black.
Mouth: Red.
Nose: Make by pinching together small section of face and working a few stitches with flesh yarn to secure shape.

THIS COMPETITION IS ALL ABOUT KNITTING.

KNITTED SIMON COWELL'S MEANEST K FACTOR MOMENTS

1. Rejecting Peter the Duck in Round 1 of the competition.

2. Rejecting Peter the Duck for a second time during Knitted Harry Hill week.

3. Splitting up newlyweds Bryan and Caroline by persuading Caroline she was better off going it alone.

KNITTED CHERYL COLE
JUDGE

MATERIALS
Patons Fab DK, approx 274m/100g ball (100% acrylic)
    1 ball in Red 2323
    1 ball in Brown 2309
Patons Fab DK, approx 68m/25g ball (100% acrylic)
    1 ball in Black 2311
Sirdar Bonus DK, approx 280m/100g ball (100% acrylic)
    1 ball in Flesh 963
Pair of 3.75mm straight needles and two double-pointed needles.
Anchor Artiste Metallic Fine Crochet Thread No 10 count, approx 250m/25g ball (65% viscose & 35% metallized polyester)
    1 ball Gold 300

Knitted Cheryl Cole featured in many of the controversial moments of the series, including an angry confrontation with Knitted Tiger Woods. Cheryl infamously told Peter the Duck that she couldn't put him through as he didn't have any wings, and later learned that her husband had been sending tapestries of himself in his pants to Winston Stimson, although she dismissed this as a "genuine mistake".

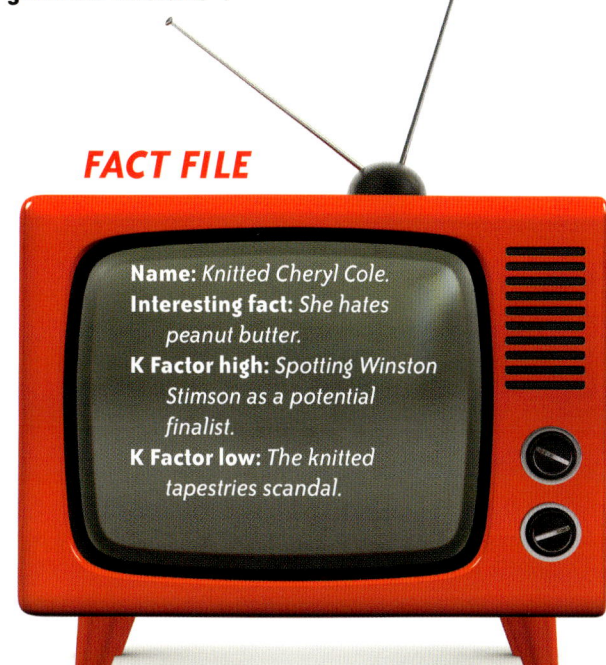

FACT FILE

Name: *Knitted Cheryl Cole.*
Interesting fact: *She hates peanut butter.*
K Factor high: *Spotting Winston Stimson as a potential finalist.*
K Factor low: *The knitted tapestries scandal.*

TENSION
23 stitches and 32 rows over 10cm stocking stitch.

SKIRT (MAKE 2)
Using 3.75mm needles and red yarn, cast on 21 sts.
Row 1: Knit.
Row 2: Purl.
Starting with a knit row, work a further 12 rows stocking stitch.
Row 15: K1, k2togtbl, knit to 3 sts, k2tog, k1. (19 sts)
Row 16: Purl.
Repeat the last 2 rows 3 more times. (13 sts)
Slip stitches onto stitch holder or spare needle – keep until added to body.

BODY (MAKE 2)
Working from the bottom upwards.
Using 3.75mm needles and flesh yarn, cast on 10 sts.
Row 1 (WS): Purl.
Row 2 (RS): K1, m1, k3, (m1, k1) twice, m1, k3, m1, k1. (15 sts)
Row 3: Purl.
Row 4: K1, m1, k13, m1, k1. (17 sts)
Repeat rows 3–4 once more. (19 sts)
Row 7: Purl.
Row 8: Knit.
Row 9: Purl.
Row 10: K1, k2togtbl, k to last 3 sts, k2tog, k1. (17 sts)
Repeat rows 7–10 twice more. (13 sts)
Row 19: Purl.
Break off flesh and join in red.
Row 20: Knit.
Row 21: Purl.
Join skirt to body on the next row as follows.
Row 22: Hold needles parallel with each other, skirt to the front. Knit across both sets of stitches with red yarn.
Row 23: Purl.
Row 24: K1, m1, k to last 3 sts, m1, k1. (15 sts)
Row 25: Purl.
Repeat rows 24–25 twice more. (19 sts)
Row 30: Knit.
Row 31: Purl.
Row 32: As row 24. (21 sts)
Work 3 rows stocking stitch.
Break off red and join in flesh.
Then work a further 4 rows stocking stitch.
Row 40: K1, k2togtbl, k to last 3 sts, k2tog, k1. (19 sts)
Work 3 rows stocking stitch.
Row 44: As row 40. (17 sts)
Row 45: Purl.
Repeat last 2 rows 4 more times until 9 sts remain.
Do not cast off – leave on spare needle.
Using mattress stitch, join side seams of body together, then join side seams of skirt together.
Thread yarn through 18 sts at neck – do not pull tight until stuffing inserted.
Next, insert ample stuffing into top and bottom openings.
Sew up bottom opening and pull thread tight at neck.
Next, using flesh-coloured yarn, secure at centre point where red and flesh change colour. Insert needle front to back a few times, and pull tight to make chest indentation.
Using picture as guide, embroider right and left pockets working Swiss darning technique.

HEAD
Using 3.75mm needles and flesh yarn, cast on 18 sts.
Row 1 (WS): Purl to end.
Row 2 (RS): K2, * m1, k2, rep from * to end. (26 sts)
Row 3: Purl.
Row 4: k3, m1,*k3, m1, rep from * to last 2 sts, k2. (34 sts)
Row 5: Purl.

Row 6: K4, m1, * k4, m1, rep from * to last 2 sts, k2. (42 sts)
Row 7: Purl.
Starting with a knit row, work a further 18 rows stocking stitch.
Row 26: k4, k2togtbl, * k3, k2togtbl, rep from * to last st k1. (34 sts)
Row 27: Purl.
Row 28: k3, k2togtbl, * k2, k2togtbl, rep from * to last st k1. (26 sts)
Row 29: Purl.
Row 30: k2, k2togtbl, * k1, k2togtbl, rep from * to last st k1. (18 sts)
Row 31: Purl.
Break off yarn, leaving a good length. Draw through remaining sts on needle and pull tight. Sew up side seam. Stuff head – sew up bottom seam and attach to body.

ARMS (MAKE 2)
Using 2 x 3.5mm double-pointed needles and flesh yarn, cast on 5 sts.
Make I-cord as follows: knit across 5 sts, do not turn, slide stitch to the RHS of needle and knit to end. Repeat this process for approx 30 rows. Cast off.

LEGS (MAKE 2)
Work legs as given above for arms for approx 40 rows. Cast off.

HAIR
Cut approx 104 lengths of brown yarn 40cm in length. Gather together 26 sections of 4 lengths. Using a crochet hook and diagram (right), attach hair to head by inserting a crochet hook under stitch. Fold section of hair in half and pull through to form a loop. Next, take the cut ends of strands through the loop and pull tight to form a tassel.

FACE
Using picture as guide, embroider face.
Eyes: Black. As French knot – wrapped around needle approx 5 times.
Mouth: Red and gold. Make heart shape.

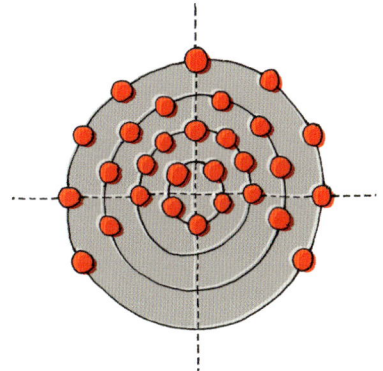

KNITTED ROLANDO OFF POPSTAR TO OPERASTAR

JUDGE

Mexican-born opera singer Knitted Rolando Off Popstar to Operastar gave his comments through the medium of song in his role as judge on The K Factor. A knitted man of few words, but plenty of high notes, Knitted Rolando's most notable moment was putting through Bessie the Dachshund, later to be one of the five finalists on the show.

MATERIALS

Patons Fab DK, approx 274m/100g ball (100% acrylic)
 1 ball in Black 2311
 1 ball in White 2306

Patons Fab DK, approx 68m/25g ball (100% acrylic)
 1 ball in Cherry 2322

Sirdar Bonus DK, approx 280m/100g ball (100% acrylic)
 1 ball in Flesh 963

Pair of 3.75mm needles

Craft Factory stick-on eyes 2 x 15mm ref. CF043

FACT FILE

Name: *Knitted Rolando Off Popstar to Operastar.*
Interesting fact: *Lives in France.*
K Factor high: *Championing Bessie the Dachshund.*
K Factor low: *Bessie the Dachshund not winning the competition.*

TENSION
23 stitches and 32 rows over 10cm stocking stitch.

BODY
Using 3.75mm needles and black yarn, cast on 28 sts.
Row 1 (WS): Purl.
Row 2 (RS): K6, m1, k2, m1, k12, m1, k2, m1, k6. (32 sts)
Row 3: Purl.
Row 4: K7, m1, k2, m1, k14, m1, k2, m1, k7. (36 sts)
Starting with a purl row, work a further 13 rows in stocking stitch.
Break off black and join in white.
Work a further 20 rows in stocking stitch ending with a purl row.

Row 38: K6, k2tog, k2, k2togtbl, k12, k2tog, k2, k2togtbl, k6. (32 sts)
Row 39: Purl.
Row 40: K5, k2tog, k2, k2togtbl, k10, k2tog, k2, k2togtbl, k5. (28 sts)
Row 41: Purl.
Row 42: K4, k2tog, k2, k2togtbl, k8, k2tog, k2, k2togtbl, k4. (24 sts)
Row 43: Purl.
Break off white and join in flesh.

HEAD
Row 44: Knit.
Row 45: Purl.
Row 46: K5, m1, k2, m1, k10, m1, k2, m1, k5. (28 sts)
Row 47: Purl.
Row 48: K6, m1, k2, m1, k12, m1, k2, m1, k6. (32 sts)
Starting with a purl row, work a further 19 rows in stocking stitch.
Break off flesh and change to black.
Row 68: K5, k2tog, k2, k2togtbl, k10, k2tog, k2, k2togtbl, k5. (28 sts)
Row 69: Purl.
Row 70: K4, k2tog, k2, k2togtbl, k8, k2tog, k2, k2togtbl, k4. (24 sts)
Row 71: Purl.
Cast off.
Sew up back and bottom seam.
Insert stuffing and sew up top seam.
Take a length of flesh-coloured yarn and thread an embroidery needle. Do not secure or tie knot. Insert needle at back seam approx 1 row from white row, and weave in and out of stitches around neck.
Pull tight and tie a double knot.
Sew in loose ends.

ARMS (MAKE 2)

Worked from top down.
Using 3.75mm needles and white yarn, cast on 12 sts.
Work 28 rows in stocking stitch.
Break off white and join in flesh.
Work 4 rows in stocking stitch.
Next row: k1, k2togtbl, knit to last 3 sts, k2tog, k1. (10 sts)
Next row: Purl.
Repeat last 2 rows once more. (8 sts)
Break off yarn, leaving a good length. Draw through remaining sts on needle and pull tight. Secure yarn and sew up side seam.

LEGS (MAKE 2)

Using 3.75mm needles and black yarn, cast on 14 sts.
Work 38 rows in stocking stitch.
Cast off.
Sew up side and bottom seams, insert stuffing and sew up top seam.
Attach arms and legs to body – use picture as guide and shaping marks on body to position arms.

HAIR

Cut approx 15 lengths of yarn approx 40cm in length in black boucle yarn.
Gather together 5 sections of 3 lengths.
Using a crochet hook and diagram (right), attach hair to head by inserting a crochet hook under stitch. Fold section of hair in half and pull through to form a loop. Next, take the cut ends of strands through the loop and pull tight to form a tassel.

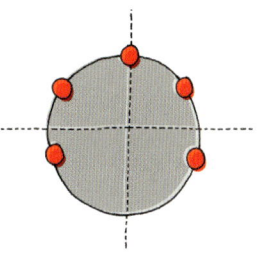

FACE

Using picture as guide, embroider face.
Eyes: 15mm sew-on toy eyes.
Mouth: Red.
Nose: Make by pinching together small section of face and working a few stitches with flesh yarn to secure shape.

TIE

Using the picture as a guide, mark with pins 2 vertical lines of stitches up the centre of the white body. Embroider using the Swiss darning technique. Alternate left and right stitches for 17 rows to create a chequered stitch pattern; then embroider both stitches for 2 rows to make the knot of the tie.

THE K FACTOR
THE ACTION FROM ROUND 2

WHO'S GOING THROUGH FROM LAST WEEK?

The knitted item from last week's K Factor going through to the Not Live Final is... Winston Stimson! The rest of you, pack your bags and get knotted!

This week on The K Factor, the judges are not in Birmingham, and the auditions are proving very popular. Sadly, Knitted Simon has not been impressed by the standard of the entries, declaring it to be one of the worst weeks they've ever had.

Then up comes a group of nine cavemen – part of a bigger prehistoric scene.

"I LIKE YOU - YOU'RE GOING THROUGH."

"IT'S A 'YES' FROM ME."

Just as things are improving, there's a security alert.

38

"I WAS JUST MAKING A PROTEST ON BEHALF OF KNITTED FATHERS FOR JUSTICE!"

PLEASE SIMON, PLEASE SIMON, PLEASE SIMON, PLEASE SIMON, PLEASE SIMON...

"DON'T LET ME DOWN, TOMMY TRUNDLE, I'M PUTTING YOU THROUGH."

Next up is Tommy Trundle the elephant, who Knitted Simon puts through after some desperate pleading.

A CHANGE OF HEART

All week, something has been nagging at Knitted Simon. Last week, he sent home a small duck called Peter – a decision that he is now regretting. With the backing of his fellow judges, Simon decides to call Peter to tell him of their change of heart.

Sadly, Peter is unable to answer Knitted Simon's call, due to the fact that he hasn't got any wings.

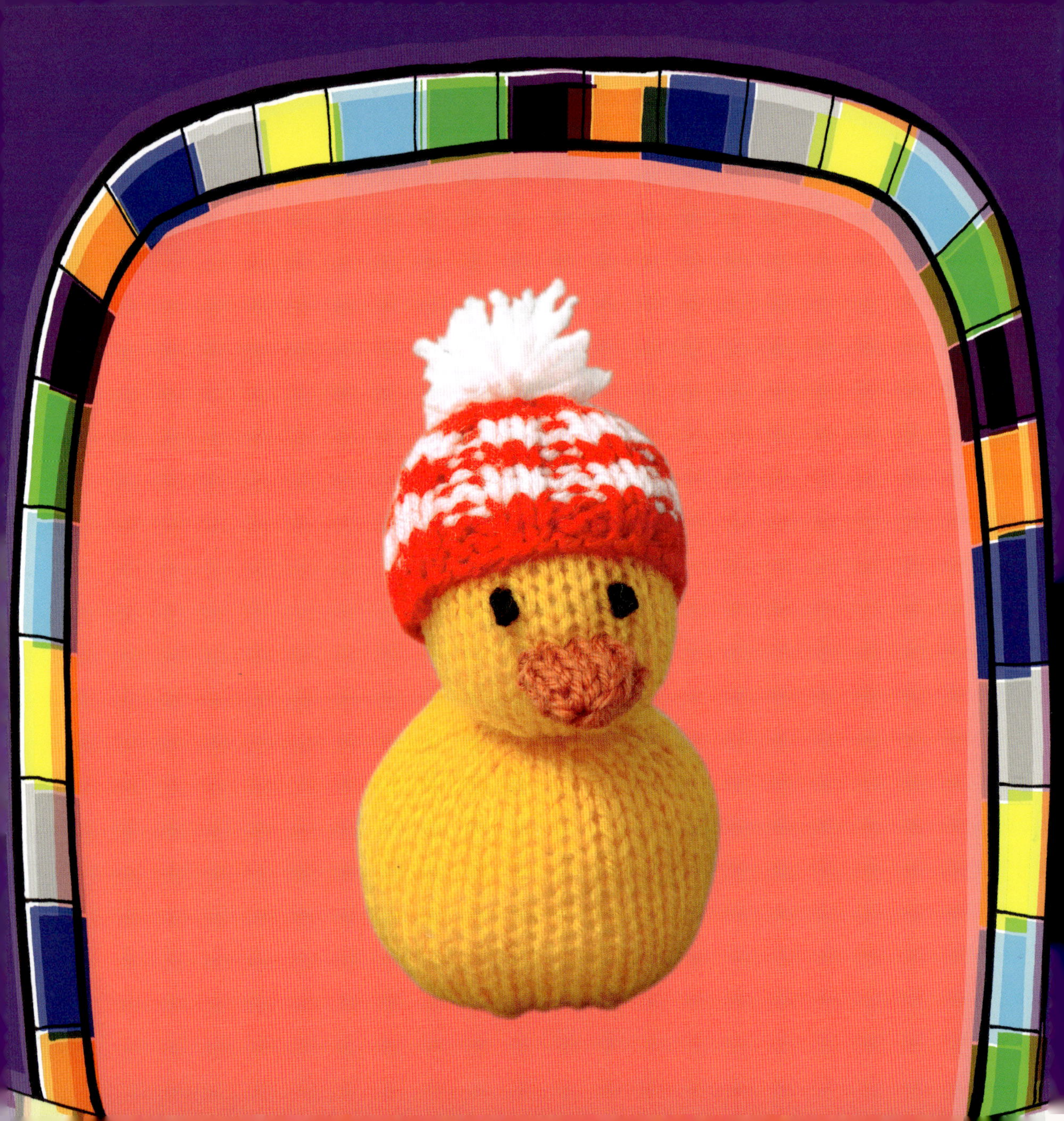

PETER THE DUCK

WINNER

Peter the Duck's K Factor journey proved to be an emotional rollercoaster. Rejected due to the fact that he didn't have any wings, and then rejected for a second time when dressed as Harry Hill, Peter's huge popularity with viewers and fellow birds alike was evident when riots broke out outside The K Factor studios demanding he be reinstated in the competition. Realising his mistake, Knitted Simon Cowell called Peter up to tell him he was putting him through after all, but wingless Peter was unable to pick up the phone. In despair, Peter attempted suicide, but was caught by Simon. During the Not Live Final – The K Factor on Ice, Peter was forced to skate on his own as there were five contestants. He was eventually crowned triumphant winner of The K Factor.

FACT FILE

Name: Peter the Duck.
Interesting fact: He lost his wings in a bizarre toaster accident.
K Factor high: Winning!
K Factor low: Attempting suicide.

IT'S NOT MY FAULT I DON'T HAVE ANY WINGS...

PETER THE DUCK'S BEST K FACTOR MOMENTS

1. His first appearance in front of the judges in Round 1.

2. Auditioning for a second time during Knitted Harry Hill Week, disguised as Harry Hill.

3. Getting a call back from Knitted Simon Cowell (although he couldn't pick up the phone because he doesn't have any wings).

4. Coming to Knitted Simon Cowell's rescue after Bryan's vicious scissor attack. Peter raced to the hospital with the pink wool needed to sew his head back on.

5. Getting support from his fans who staged a protest outside The K Factor studios.

6. Being saved by Knitted Simon Cowell after plummeting from a cliff.

7. Skating to victory in the Not Live Final: The K Factor on Ice, despite not having any wings.

43

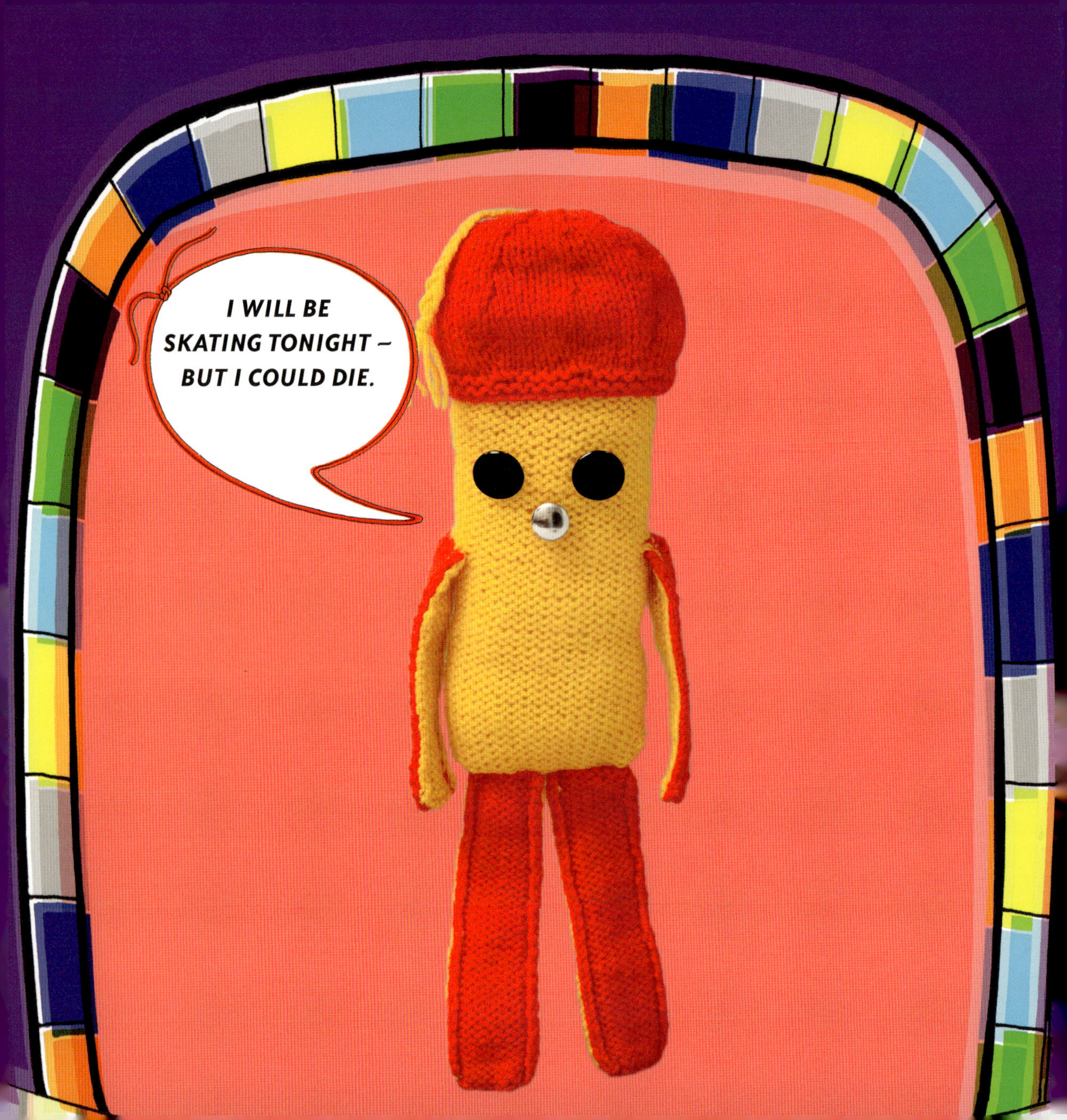
I WILL BE SKATING TONIGHT – BUT I COULD DIE.

WINSTON STIMSON

FINALIST

Winston Stimson was knitted by Linda Stimson for her 10-year-old grandson, George, as an example of an old-fashioned toy for his school project about World War II. Winston confessed to Knitted Simon Cowell that his motivation to win the competition was that he wanted a copy of the TV Burp book, but couldn't be bothered to buy one. After revealing a tragic back-story in which he was accidentally put in the washing machine by his mum, the judges put him through. Winston was to hit the headlines the following week, when he became embroiled in a scandal involving Knitted Cheryl's husband, Knitted Ashley, who sent tapestries of himself in his underpants to Winston. The drama continued when, during the rehearsals for The K Factor on Ice, Winston fell awkwardly and broke his leg. Not wanting to let his fans down, Winston vowed to go on, performing a stunning routine to Ravel's "Boléro" with Bessie the Dachshund as his skating partner.

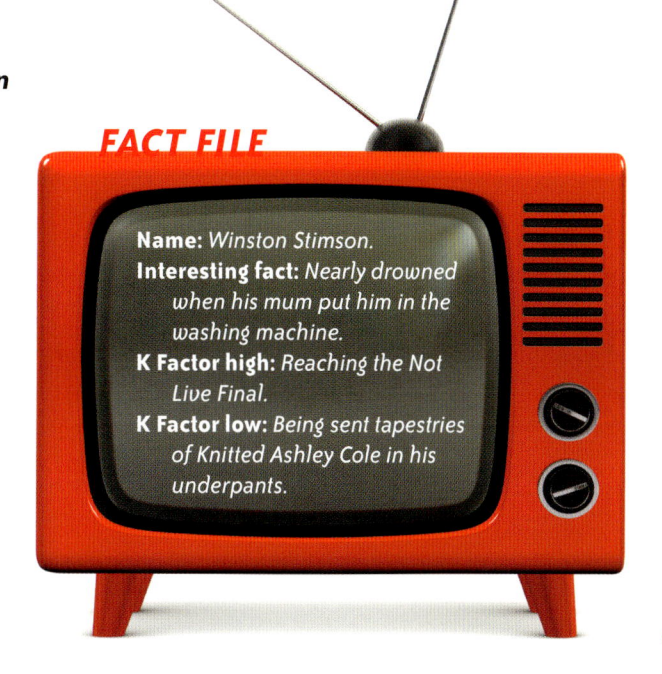

FACT FILE

Name: Winston Stimson.
Interesting fact: Nearly drowned when his mum put him in the washing machine.
K Factor high: Reaching the Not Live Final.
K Factor low: Being sent tapestries of Knitted Ashley Cole in his underpants.

MATERIALS
Patons Fab DK, approx 274m/100g ball (100% acrylic)
    1 ball in Canary 2305
    1 ball in Red 2323
Pair of 3.75mm needles

Two 20mm black metal shanks
One 15mm Prym Metal cover button

TENSION
23 stitches and 32 rows over 10cm stocking stitch.

BODY
Worked in reverse stocking stitch throughout.
Using 3.75mm needles and canary yarn, cast on 38 sts.
Work in reverse stocking stitch for 62 rows.
Cast off.
Sew up side and bottom seam.
Insert stuffing to make slightly padded – use picture as guide to get correct shape.
Sew up top seam.

LEGS
Make 4: 2 red (fronts), 2 canary (backs)
Make each section as below.
Cast on 8 sts.
Work in rev st st for 40 rows.
Cast off.
With knit sides together stitch around sides top and bottom.

ARMS
Make 4: 2 red (fronts), 2 canary (backs)
Make each section as below.
Cast on 6 sts.
Work in rev st st for 34 rows.
Cast off.
With knit sides together, stitch around sides top and bottom.
Using picture as guide, sew legs and arms to body.

HAT
Using 3.75mm needles and red yarn, cast on 40 sts.
Row 1: Knit.
Row 2: Knit.
Repeat last 2 rows once more.
Row 5: K3, m1*, k5, m1, rep from * to last 2 sts, k2. (48 sts)
Row 6: Purl.
Row 7: K4, m1*, k6, m1, rep from * to last 2 sts, k2. (56 sts)
Row 8: Purl.
Row 9: K5, m1*, k7, m1, rep from * to last 2 sts, k2. (64 sts)
Beginning with a purl row, work 3 rows stocking stitch.
Row 13: K4, k2tog, *k6, k2tog, rep from * to last 2 sts, k2. (56 sts)
Beginning with a purl row, work 3 rows stocking stitch.
Row 17: K3, k2tog, *k5, k2tog, rep from * to last 2 sts, k2. (48 sts)
Beginning with a purl row, work 3 rows stocking stitch.
Row 21: K2, k2tog, *k4, k2tog, rep from * to last 2 sts, k2. (40 sts)
Beginning with a purl row, work 3 rows stocking stitch.
Row 25: K1, k2tog, *k3, k2tog, rep from * to last 2 sts, k2. (32 sts)
Row 26: Purl.
Row 27: K1, k2tog, * k2, k2tog, rep from * to last st, k1. (24 sts)
Row 28: Purl.

Row 29: K2, * k2tog, k1, rep from * to last st, k1. (17 sts)
Row 30: Purl.
Row 31: K1, * k2tog, rep from * to last 2 sts, k2. (10 sts)
Row 32: Purl.
Break off yarn and thread through sts on needle, pull tight and secure. Sew down side seam.

Tassel
Cut 3 lengths of yarn approx 40cm each.
Thread through top of hat so you have 6 equal lengths. Plait together to approx 11cm long. Tie a knot to secure. Using picture as guide, sew buttons onto face for eyes and nose.

MY MUM PUT ME IN THE WASHING MACHINE AND I NEARLY DROWNED.

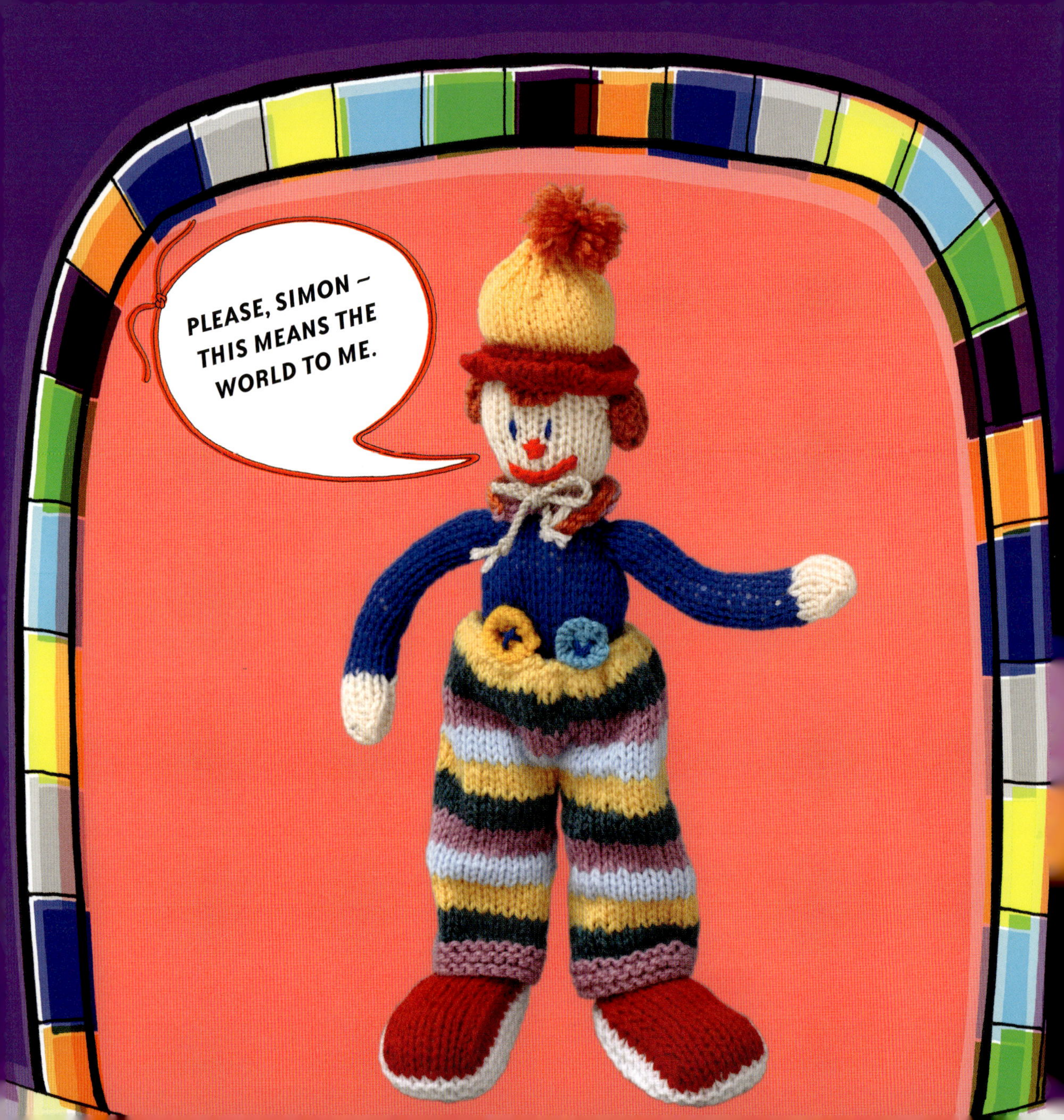
PLEASE, SIMON – THIS MEANS THE WORLD TO ME.

NINJA CLOWN

MATERIALS
Sirdar Bonus DK, approx 280m/100g ball (100% acrylic)
   1 ball in Flesh 963
Patons Diploma Gold DK, approx 125m/50g ball (55% wool, 45% acrylic)
   1 ball in Bright Aqua 6243
Sirdar Country Style DK, approx 318m/100g ball (45% acrylic, 40% nylon, 15% wool)
   1 ball in Gemini 502
   1 ball in Sweet Cicely Pink 587
Patons Fab DK, approx 68m/25g ball (100% acrylic)
   1 ball in Blue 2321
   1 ball in Yellow 2302
   1 ball in Cherry 2322
   1 ball in Red 2323
   1 ball in White 2306
Adriafil Regina DK, approx 120m/50g ball (100% pure wool)
   1 ball in Orange 35
Sirdar Country Style DK, approx 175m/50g ball (100% acrylic)
   1 ball in Pastel Blue 321
Elastic thread

Ninja Clown's chances of progressing in the competition seemed bleak when Knitted Simon Cowell told him that he didn't like his hat. However, the jovial clown's impassioned plea seemed to resonate with the judges, and he was put through. Sadly, he failed to connect with the viewers of the show, and wasn't voted through to the Not Live Final.

FACT FILE

Name: *Ninja Clown.*
Interesting fact: *He's from Weston-super-Mare.*
K Factor high: *Getting through the first round of the competition.*
K Factor low: *Simon's harsh hat comments.*

TENSION
23 stitches and 32 rows over 10cm stocking stitch.

BODY
Using 3.75mm needle and blue yarn, cast on 24 sts.
Row 1 (WS): Purl.
Row 2 (RS): K5, m1, k2, m1, k10, m1, k2, m1, k5. (28 sts).
Row 3: Purl.
Row 4: K6, m1, k2, m1, k12, m1, k2, m1, k6. (32 sts)
Starting with a purl row, work a further 13 rows in stocking stitch.
Row 18: K5, k2tog, k2, k2togtbl, k10, k2tog, k2, k2togtbl, k5. (28 sts)
Row 19: Purl.
Row 20: K4, k2tog, k2, k2togtbl, k8, k2tog, k2, k2togtbl, k4. (24 sts)
Row 21: Purl.
Break off blue, join in flesh.
Row 22: K3, k2tog, k2, k2togtbl, k6, k2tog, k2, k2togtbl, k3. (20 sts)
Row 23: Purl.

HEAD
Row 1: K6, k2togtbl, k4, k2tog, k6. (18 sts)
Row 2: Purl.
Row 3: K4, m1, k2, m1, k6, m1, k2, m1, k4. (22 sts)
Row 4: Purl.
Row 5: K5, m1, k2, m1, k8, m1, k2, m1, k5. (26 sts)
Starting with a purl row, work a further 11 rows in stocking stitch.
Row 17: K4, k2tog, k2, k2togtbl, k6, k2tog, k2, k2togtbl, k4. (22 sts)
Row 18: Purl.
Row 19: K3, k2tog, k2, k2togtbl, k4, k2tog, k2, k2togtbl, k3. (18 sts)

Row 20: Purl.
Cast off.
Sew up back and bottom seam.
Insert stuffing and sew up top seam.
Take a length of flesh-coloured yarn and thread an embroidery needle. Do not secure or tie knot. Insert needle at back seam approx 4 rows from blue row and weave in and out of stitches around neck.
Pull tight and tie a double knot.
Sew in loose ends.

ARMS (MAKE 2)
Worked from the top down.
Using 3.75mm needles and blue yarn, cast on 8 sts.
Starting with a knit row, work 20 rows in stocking stitch.
Knit the next 4 rows.
Break off blue and join in flesh.
Work next 6 rows in stocking stitch.
Break off yarn and thread through sts on needle, pull tight and secure.
Sew up side seam.
Insert stuffing, and then sew up top seam. Stitch into position on body, using shaping marks on body as guide.

LEGS (MAKE 2)
Using 3.75mm needles and flesh yarn, cast on 9 sts.
Starting with a knit row, work 30 rows in stocking stitch.
Row 31: K1, m1, k7, m1, k1. (11 sts)
Starting with a purl row, work 3 rows stocking stitch.
Row 35: K1, m1, k9, m1, k1. (13 sts)
Row 36: Purl.
Cast off.
Sew up side seam of leg.
Insert stuffing, and then sew up top seam. Stitch into position on body.

SHOES (MAKE 2)

Using 3.75mm needles and white yarn, cast on 16 sts.

Row 1: K1, yfwd, k6, yfwd, k1, yfwd, k1, yfwd, k6, yfwd, k1. (21 sts)

Row 2: K1, ktbl next st, k6, ktbl next st, k1, ktbl next st, k1, ktbl next st, k6, ktbl next st, k1.

Row 3: K1, yfwd, k7, yfwd, k2, yfwd, k3, yfwd, k7, yfwd, k1. (26 sts)

Row 4: K1, ktbl next st, k7, ktbl next st, k3, ktbl next st, k2, ktbl next st, k7, ktbl next st, k1.

Row 5: K1, yfwd, k8, yfwd, k4, yfwd, k4, yfwd, k8, yfwd, k1. (31 sts)

Row 6: K1, ktbl next st, k8, ktbl next st, k4, ktbl next st, k4, ktbl next st, k7, ktbl next st, k1.

Row 7: K1, yfwd, k9, yfwd, k5, yfwd, k6, yfwd, k9, yfwd, k1. (36 sts)

Row 8: K1, ktbl next st, k9, ktbl next st, k5, ktbl next st, k6, ktbl next st, k9, ktbl next st, k1.

Row 9: Knit.

Row 10: Knit.

Break off white and join in red.

Row 11: Knit.

Row 12: Purl.

Shape top of shoe as follows.

Knit until 15 sts on LHN, K2togtbl * turn, Sl 1st st, P6, P2tog, turn, Sl 1st st, k6, k2togtbl, rep from * until 5 sts on LHN, turn, Sl 1st st, p6, p2tog, turn Sl 1st st, knit to end.

Cast off knitwise.

Sew up back seam and sole.

Cut sole shape out of cardboard using template (right) and insert into shoe.

Insert ample stuffing, leaving a small space for leg to fit into; insert leg and stitch into place.

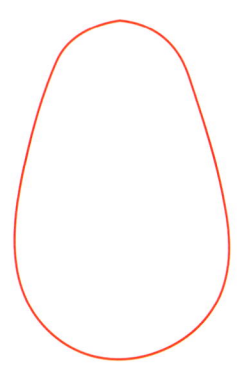

TROUSERS
Legs (make 2)
Work each leg separately from the waist in the following stripe sequence:
Rows 1–4: Pastel blue.
Rows 5–8: Yellow.
Rows 9–12: Gemini.
Rows 13–16: Sweet cicely pink.
Cast on 30 sts.
Starting with a knit row, work 5 rows stocking stitch.
Next row: Knit.
Starting with a purl row work in stocking stitch for a further 41 rows, keeping stripe sequence correct.
Work 5 rows in knit.
Cast off knitwise.
Break off yarn.
Sew side seams of legs together from the bottom up to row 21 on each leg.
Join left and right legs together front and back from row 20 to row 1.
Fold the top of the trousers over at row 6 and stitch to form waist band.
Using elastic thread, weave in and out of stitches on row 3.
Place trousers on body, pull ends of elastic tight around the body and tie knot to secure.

HAIR
Using 3.75mm needles and orange yarn, cast on 8 sts.
Row 1: Knit.
Row 2: K4,* m1, k1, rep from * to end. (12 sts)
Work the next 29 rows in knit.
Row 32: K3, * k2tog to last st, k1.
Cast off.
Fold in half to form long tube and sew up long edge.
Sew one end seam, then insert stuffing; sew up open end.
Pin and stitch onto head.
Fringe
Using 3.75mm needles and orange yarn, cast on 4 sts.
Work 4 rows knit.
Cast off.
Place on the head so the rows are running vertically and stitch into place.

COLLAR
Using 3.75mm needle and pink yarn, cast on 18 sts.
Row 1 (WS): K1, p16, k1.
Row 2 (RS): K2, * m1, k2, rep from * to end (26 sts).
Row 3: K1, p to last st, k1.
Break off pink and join in orange.
Row 4: Knit.
Cast off.
Sew in loose ends.
Collar ties
Make twisted cord approx 15cm using beige yarn.
Place collar around neck and then thread cord through 1st and last st on cast-on edge.
Tie into a bow.

BUTTONS (MAKE 2)
Using bright aqua yarn and 3.75mm needles, cast on 18 sts.
Row 1: K1, *k2tog, rep from * to last st, k1. (10 sts)
Row 2: P1, * p2tog, rep from * to last st, p1. (6 sts)
Break off yarn and thread through sts on needle, pull tight and sew up side seam to form a small circle.
Sew in loose ends.
Make another button as above using yellow yarn.
Stitch into position on body directly above trousers.

HAT

Using 3.75mm needle and cherry yarn, cast on 34 sts.
Row 1 (WS): Purl.
Row 2 (RS): K5, m1, * k4, m1, rep from * to last st, k1. (42 sts)
Row 3: Knit.
Row 4: Knit.
Row 5: K3, k2tog, * k2, k2tog, rep from * to last st, k1. (32 sts)
Row 6: Purl.
Work 3 rows knit.
Break off red and join in yellow.
Starting with a knit row, work a further 8 rows stocking stitch.
Row 18: K2, * k2tog, k1, rep from * to end. (22 sts)
Row 19: Purl.
Row 20: K1, * k2tog, rep from * to last st, k1 (12 sts).
Row 21: Purl.
Row 22: K1, * K2tog, rep from * to last st, k1. (7 sts)
Break off yarn and thread through sts on needle, pull tight and secure.
Sew side seams of hat together.
Fold over brim at row 3, stitch into place.
Make small pom-pom with orange yarn and attach to top of hat.
Sew hat onto head.

FACE

Using picture as guide, embroider face.
Eyes: Blue. As French knot – wrapped around needle approx 5 times.
Mouth: Red. Chain stitch.
Nose: Red. Satin stitch.

THE K FACTOR
THE ACTION FROM ROUND 3

WHO'S GOING THROUGH FROM LAST WEEK?

The knitted item safe and coming back to the Not Live Final is... Tommy Trundle! The rest of you, get knotted!

It's Knitted Harry Hill Week on The K Factor, and all the contestants have been invited to dress up as Harry Hill.

Little do the contestants know that, as a special surprise for them, Knitted Simon Cowell has arranged for the Real Knitted Harry Hill to take time out from his TV Burp to come down to the studio to meet them.

The Knitted Harrys go in front of the judges one by one. Competition is fierce.

CHERYL'S BOMBSHELL

This week, Knitted Cheryl Cole receives a bombshell. A tabloid newspaper has printed a story about her husband, Knitted Ashley, alleging that he has been knitting tapestries of himself in his pants and sending them to Winston Stimson.

IT WAS A GENUINE MISTAKE.

In an interview with Piers Morgan, Winston admits that he is "deeply embarrassed" by the story, and apologises to all his fans.

Knitted Simon thinks he recognises one of the Knitted Harrys. Peter the Duck, dressed as Harry Hill, tries again, but he is unsuccessful.

"YOU LOOK FAMILIAR. HAVE WE MET BEFORE? IT'S A 'NO', I'M AFRAID."

"YOU DON'T LOOK ANYTHING LIKE HIM, PET."

55

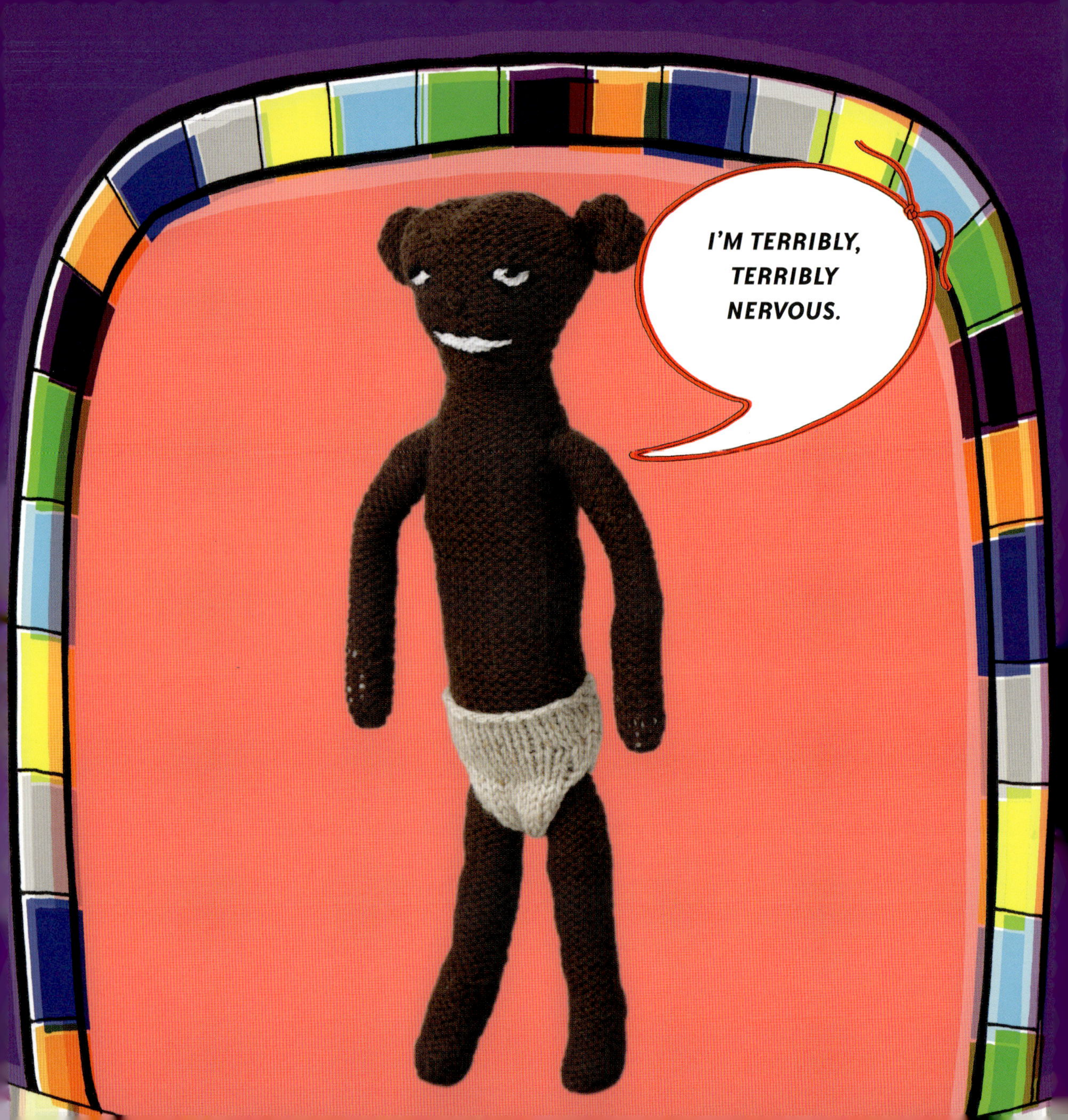
I'M TERRIBLY, TERRIBLY NERVOUS.

PHILNUT

Auditioning in Round 1 of The K Factor, Philnut's choice of outfit seemed to confuse the judges. Knitted Simon Cowell was keen to know why he was only wearing pants. Philnut explained that it was because he was worried that, if he wore a suit, he'd "get egged". Impressed by his potential, Simon declared that he thought Philnut could go a long way in the competition. Unfortunately, the public didn't agree, and Philnut failed to reach the Not Live Final.

MATERIALS
Sirdar Country Style DK, approx 318m/100g ball (45% acrylic, 40% nylon, 15% wool)
    1 ball in Chocolate 530
    1 ball in Hopsack 597
Patons Fab DK, approx 68m/25g ball (100% acrylic)
    1 ball in White 2306
    1 ball in Black 2311
Pair of 3.75mm needles

FACT FILE
Name: Philnut.
Interesting fact: He's from Norwich.
K Factor high: Getting a "yes" from Knitted Simon Cowell.
K Factor low: Appearing onstage in his underwear.

TENSION

23 stitches and 32 rows over 10cm stocking stitch.

BODY

Worked in reverse stocking stitch throughout.
Using 3.75mm needles and chocolate yarn, cast on 24 sts.
Row 1 (RS): Purl.
Row 2 (WS): Knit.
Row 3: P5, m1, p2, m1, p10, m1, p2, m1, p5. (28 sts)
Starting with a knit row, work in rev st st for 3 rows.
Row 7: P6, m1, p2, m1, p12, m1, p2, m1, p6. (32 sts)
Starting with a knit row, work in rev st st for 31 rows.
Row 39: P5, p2tog, p2, p2tog, p10, p2tog, p2, p2tog, p5. (28 sts)
Row 40: Knit.
Row 41: P4, p2tog, p2, p2tog, p8, p2tog, p2, p2tog, p4. (24 sts)
Row 42: Knit.
Row 43: P3, p2tog, p2, p2tog, p6, p2tog, p2, p2tog, p3. (20 sts)
Row 44: Knit.

HEAD

Row 45: Purl.
Row 46: Knit.
Row 47: P4, m1, m2, m1, p8, m1, p2, m1, p4. (24 sts)
Row 48: Knit.
Work next row as follows using short row shaping technique to create chin.
Row 49: P5, m1, p2, m1, p8, turn, slp 1, k5, turn, sl1, p7, turn, sl1, k9, turn, sl1, p9, m1, p2, m1, p5. (28 sts)
Row 50: Knit.
Row 51: P6, m1, p2, m1, p12, m1, p2, m1, p6. (32 sts)
Row 52: Knit.
Row 53: P7, m1, p2, m1, p14, m1, p2, m1, p7. (36 sts)
Starting with a knit row, work in rev st st for 3 rows.
Row 57: P8, m1, p2, m1, p16, m1, p2, m1, p8. (38 sts)
Starting with a knit row, work in rev st st for 5 rows.
Row 63: P8, (p2tog) twice, p16, (p2tog) twice, p8. (36 sts)
Row 64: K7, (k2tog) twice, k14, (k2tog) twice, k7. (32 sts)
Row 65: P6, (p2tog) twice, p12, (p2tog) twice, p6. (28 sts)
Row 66: K5, (k2tog) twice, k10, (k2tog) twice, k5. (24 sts)
Row 67: P4, (p2tog) twice, p8, (p2tog) twice, p4. (20 sts)
Cast off.
Break off yarn, sew down back seam and bottom.
Insert stuffing from top – using picture as guide to create correct shape; sew up top seam.

LEGS (MAKE 2)

Using 3.75mm needles and chocolate yarn, cast on 14 sts.
Work in reverse stocking stitch for 40 rows.
Cast off.
Sew up side seam and bottom – purl side is right side.
Insert stuffing and sew up top seam.

ARMS (MAKE 2)

Using 3.75mm needles and chocolate yarn, cast on 12 sts.
Work in reverse stocking stitch for 34 rows.
Break off yarn and thread through sts on needle; pull tight and secure.
Sew up side seam and bottom – purl side is right side.
Insert stuffing and sew up top seam.

EARS (MAKE 2)

Using 3.75mm needles and chocolate yarn, cast on 12 sts.
Row 1 (RS): Purl.
Row 2 (WS): Knit.
Work 8 rows of reverse stocking stitch.
Row 11: *P2tog, rep from * to end.
Break off yarn and thread through sts on needle, pull tight and sew into position on head.

PANTS

Using 3.75mm needles and hopsack yarn, cast on 16 sts.
Row 1 (RS): Knit.
Row 2 (WS): Purl.
Repeat rows 1–2 once more.
Row 5: K1, k2togtbl, k to last 3 sts, k2tog, k1. (14 sts)
Beginning with a purl row, work 3 rows stocking stitch.
Row 9: As row 5. (12 sts)
Beginning with a purl row, work 5 rows stocking stitch.
Row 15: As row 5. (10 sts)
Row 16: Purl to end.
Row 17: As row 5. (8 sts)
Beginning with a purl row, work 3 rows stocking stitch.
Row 21: K1, m1, knit to last st, m1, k1. (10 sts)
Row 22: Purl.
Row 23: As row 21. (12 sts)
Beginning with a purl row, work 5 rows stocking stitch.
Row 29: As row 21. (14 sts)
Beginning with a purl row, work 3 rows stocking stitch.
Row 33: As row 21. (16 sts)
Beginning with a purl row, work 3 rows stocking stitch.
Cast off.
Fold in half and sew up side seams from top to approx half way.
Place on doll and stitch into place.

FACE

Using picture as guide, embroider face.
Nose: Make by pinching together a small section of face and working a few stitches with chocolate brown yarn to secure the shape.
Eyes: White satin stitch, outlined in black backstitch, with French knots for the pupils.
Mouth: White long, horizontal straight stitches, outlined in black backstitch.

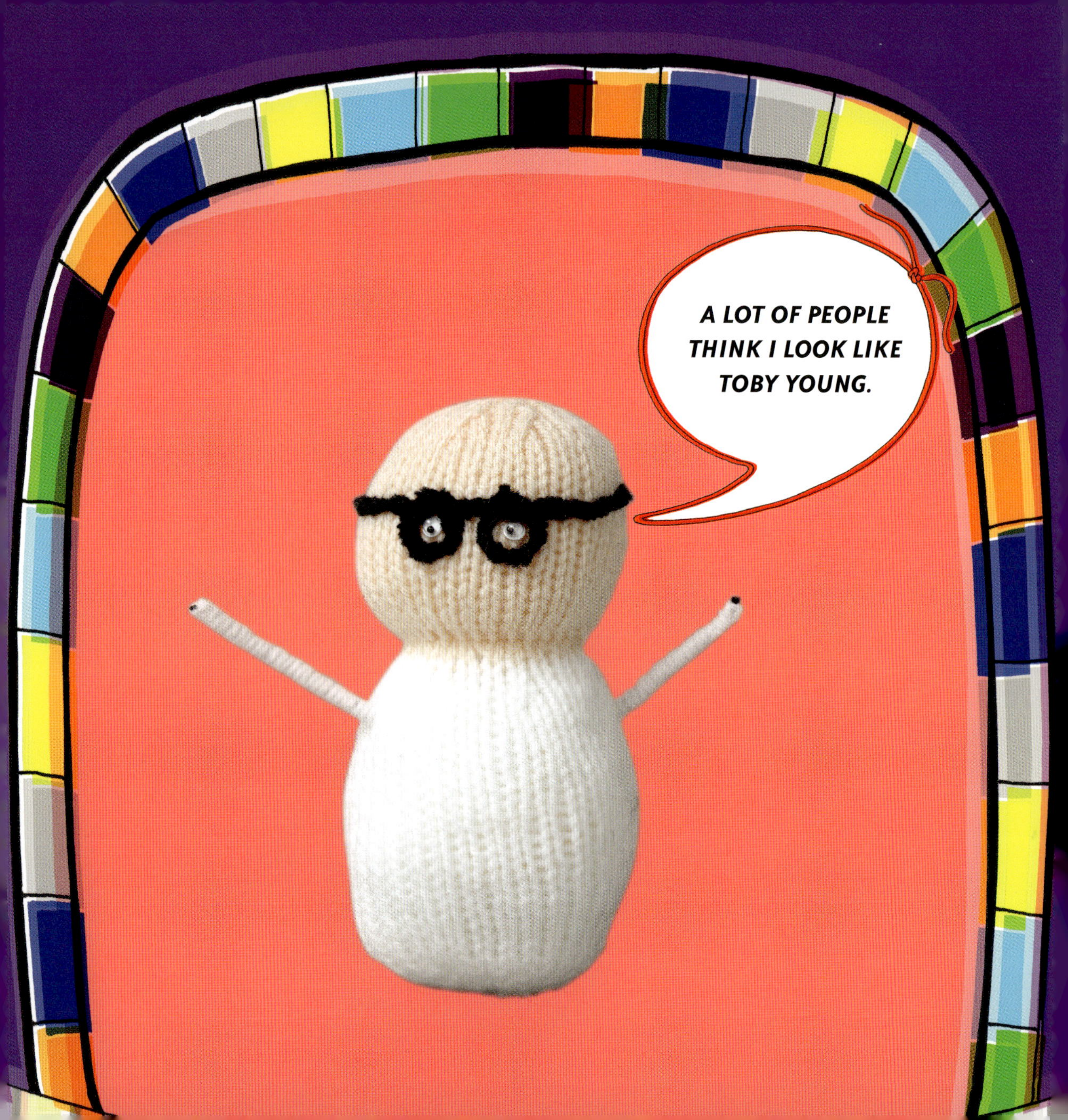
A LOT OF PEOPLE THINK I LOOK LIKE TOBY YOUNG.

GARY

Gary from Lincoln appeared in the opening round of The K Factor. Knitted Cheryl Cole told him that he reminded her of someone, and Gary confirmed that people often thought that he resembled the journalist and author, Toby Young. Gary greatly impressed the judges – in particular, The Knitted Character, who declared, "You're coming to London, Gary!"

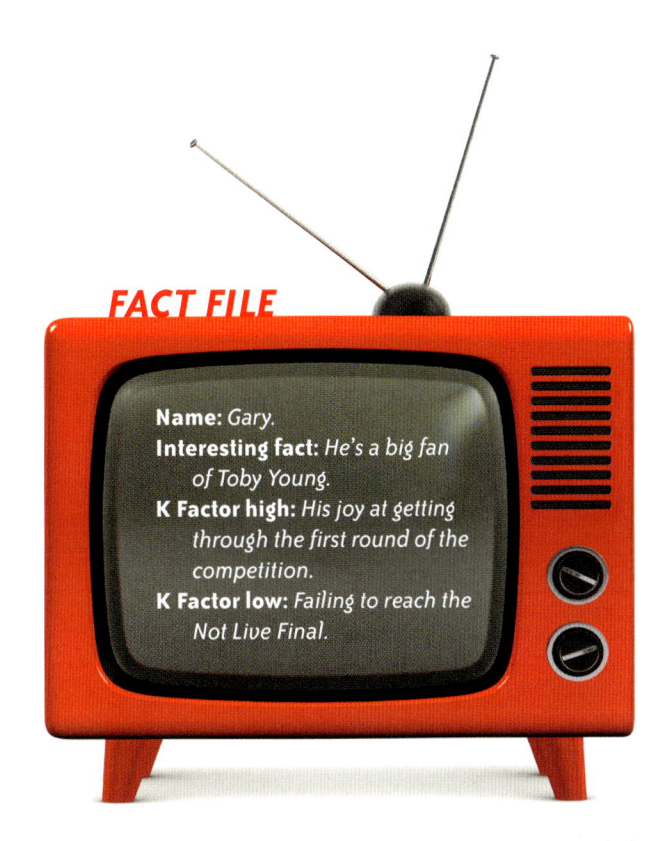

FACT FILE

Name: *Gary.*
Interesting fact: *He's a big fan of Toby Young.*
K Factor high: *His joy at getting through the first round of the competition.*
K Factor low: *Failing to reach the Not Live Final.*

MATERIALS

Patons Fab DK, approx 68m/25g ball (100% acrylic)
   1 ball in White 2306
   1 ball in Black 2311
Sirdar Bonus DK, approx 280m/100g ball (100% acrylic)
   1 ball in Flesh 963
Pair of 3.75mm needles

One black pipe cleaner
Craft Factory stick-on eyes
   2 x 3mm ref. CF035

TENSION

23 stitches and 32 rows over 10cm stocking stitch.

BODY

Using 3.75mm needles and white yarn, cast on 10 sts.
Row 1 (WS): Purl.
Row 2 (RS): K2, * M1, K1, rep from * to end. (18 sts)
Row 3: Purl.
Row 4: K3, * M1, K2, rep from * to last st, k1. (26 sts)
Row 5: Purl.
Row 6: K4, m1,* k3, m1, rep from * to last st, k1. (34 sts)
Starting with a purl row, work in stocking stitch for a further 23 rows.
Row 30: K2, *k2tog, k2, rep from * to end. (26 sts)
Row 31: Purl.
Break off white yarn and join in flesh.

HEAD

Row 1: Knit.
Row 2: Purl.
Row 3: K4, m1, * k3, m1, rep from * to last st, k1. (34 sts)
Starting with a purl row, work in stocking stitch for a further 19 rows.
Row 23: K2, *k2tog, k2, rep from * to end. (26 sts)
Row 24: Purl.
Row 25: K1, * k2tog, k1, rep from * to last st, k1. (18 sts)
Row 26: Purl.
Row 27: K1, * k2tog, rep from * to last st, k1. (10 sts)
Row 28: Purl.
Break off yarn and thread through sts on needle, pull tight and secure. Sew up back seam.
Insert stuffing – using picture as guide to achieve the correct shape. Sew up bottom seam.
Take a length of flesh-coloured yarn and thread an embroidery needle. Do not secure or tie knot. Insert needle at back seam approx 3 rows from white row and weave in and out of stitches around neck.
Pull tight and tie a double knot.
Sew in loose ends.

ARMS

Cut pipe cleaner to approx 15cm.
Wrap white yarn around pipe cleaner; alternatively, if you find this tricky, just use a white pipe cleaner.
Insert a knitting needle approx 2cm from neck and poke straight through from side to side for the arms; wiggle needle around to make a hole through the body; remove needle and insert pipe cleaner arms through the hole.
Stitch arms to body using white yarn to secure them – bend into shape.

GLASSES

Take black pipe cleaner and, at approx the halfway mark, wrap around your little finger to create a loop; repeat this so you have 2 circles in the centre.
Make sure both circles are the same size.
Position on head, using picture as guide.
Stitch into place using black yarn.
Carefully peel off backing from eyes and stick onto head at the centre of the glasses.

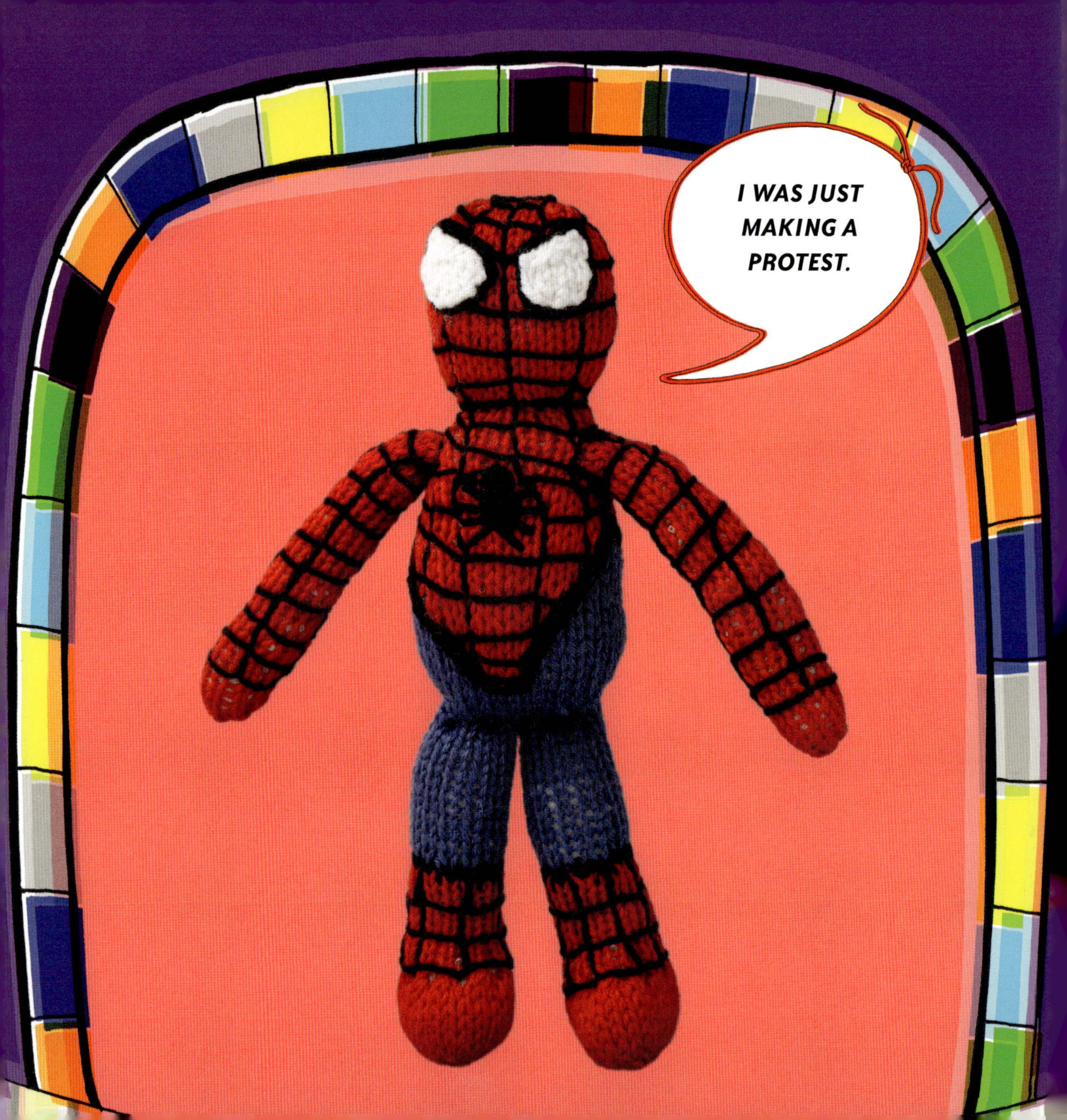
I WAS JUST MAKING A PROTEST.

KNITTED SPIDER-MAN

Knitted Spider-Man is a Knitted Fathers For Justice protester who famously invaded The K Factor studio during Round 2 of the competition, causing a major security alert. He was quickly detained by security and escorted out of the building, but not before making an impassioned plea on behalf of Knitted Fathers For Justice. Knitted Spider-Man was to reappear in the final episode of The K Factor, playing a stunning guitar solo during the contestants' rendition of "Don't Stop Believin'".

MATERIALS

Patons Diploma Gold DK, approx 125m/50g ball (55% wool, 45% acrylic)
    1 ball in Red 6151
    1 ball in Airforce 6169
Patons Fab DK, approx 68m/25g ball (100% acrylic)
    1 ball in White 2306
    1 ball in Black 2311
Pair of 3.75mm needles

FACT FILE

Name: *Knitted Spider-Man.*
Interesting fact: *He spins his own yarns and threads.*
K Factor high: *Publicity for his cause, Knitted Fathers For Justice.*
K Factor low: *Being manhandled by security.*

TENSION
23 stitches and 32 rows over 10cm stocking stitch.

BODY
Using 3.75mm needles and Airforce yarn, cast on 24 sts.
Row 1: Purl.
Row 2: K5, m1, k2, m1, k10, m1, k2, m1, k5. (28 sts)
Row 3: Purl.
Row 4: K6, m1, k2, m1, k12, m1, k2, m1, k6. (32 sts)
Row 5: Purl.
Work next 14 rows in Airforce and red from graph (below) using the intarsia technique.
Break off Airforce, and work in red yarn.
Row 20: K5, k2tog, k2, k2togtbl, k10, k2tog, k2, k2togtbl, k5. (28 sts)
Row 21: Purl.
Row 22: K4, k2tog, k2, k2togtbl, k8, k2tog, k2, k2togtbl, k4. (24 sts)
Row 23: Purl.
Row 24: K3, k2tog, k2, k2togtbl, k6, k2tog, k2, k2togtbl, k3. (20 sts)
Row 25: Purl.

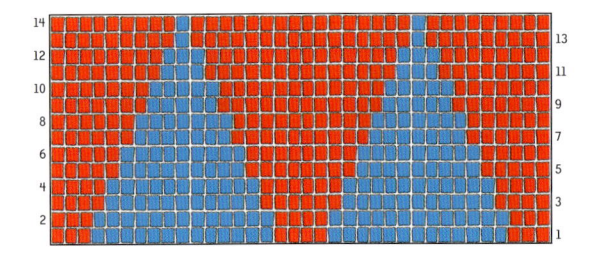

HEAD
Row 1: K6, k2togtbl, k4, k2tog, k6. (18 sts)
Row 2: Purl.
Row 3: K4, m1, k2, m1, k6, m1, k2, m1, k4. (22 sts)
Row 4: Purl.
Row 5: K5, m1, k2, m1, k8, m1, k2, m1, k5. (26 sts)
Starting with a purl row, work a further 11 rows in stocking stitch.
Row 17: K4, k2tog, k2, k2togtbl, k6, k2tog, k2, k2togtbl, k4. (22 sts)
Row 18: Purl.
Row 19: K3, k2tog, k2, k2togtbl, k4, k2tog, k2, k2togtbl, k3. (18 sts)
Row 20: Purl.
Cast off.
Sew up back and bottom seam, insert stuffing, then sew up top seam.
Take a length of red yarn and thread an embroidery needle. Do not secure or tie knot. Insert needle at back seam at approx 2nd row of head and weave in and out of stitches around neck.
Pull tight and tie a double knot.
Sew in loose ends.

LEGS (MAKE 2)
Using 3.75mm needles and red yarn, cast on 16 sts.
Row 1: K1, * k1, m1, rep from * to last st, k1. (30 sts)
Starting with a purl row, work 5 rows in stocking stitch.
Row 7: K3, * k3tog, rep from * to last 3 sts, k3. (14 sts)
Starting with a purl row, work 9 rows in stocking stitch.
Break off red and join in Airforce.
Starting with a purl row, work 13 rows in stocking stitch.
Cast off.
Sew up back seam and sole.
Insert stuffing, and then sew up top opening.

ARMS (MAKE 2)
Worked from top down.
Using 3.75mm needles and red yarn, cast on 12 sts.
Work 32 rows in stocking stitch.
Next row: k1, k2togtbl, knit to last 3 sts, k2tog, k1. (10 sts)
Next row: Purl.
Repeat last 2 rows once more. (8 sts)
Break off yarn, leaving a good length. Draw through remaining sts on needle and pull tight. Secure yarn and sew up side seam. Insert stuffing and sew up top seam. Attach arms and legs to body using picture and shaping marks on body for arms.

RIGHT EYE
Using 3.25mm needles and white yarn, cast on 3 sts.
Row 1 (RS): Knit into front and back of 1st st, k1, knit into front and back of last st. (5 sts)
Row 2 (WS): Purl into back and front of next st, purl to end. (6 sts)
Row 3: Knit to end.
Row 4: Cast off 3 sts knitwise, purl to end of row.
Row 5: K1, k2tog. (2 sts)
Row 6: P2tog.
Break off yarn and thread through last st.

LEFT EYE
Using 3.25mm needles and white yarn, cast on 3 sts.
Row 1 (WS): Purl into back and front of 1st st, p1, purl into back and front of last st. (5 sts)
Row 2 (RS): Knit into front and back of 1st st, knit to end. (6 sts)
Row 3: Purl to end.
Row 4: Cast off 3 sts purlwise, knit to end of row.
Row 5: P1, p2tog. (2 sts)
Row 6: K2tog.
Break off yarn and thread through last st.
Attach eyes to head, using the picture as guide.

MARKINGS
Using picture as guide, embroider body and head.
Work 1 row of backstitch around the outside of both eyes using black yarn.
Embroider spider onto centre of chest using black yarn and satin stitch.
Embroider rest of body as follows.
Starting at the top of the head, using black yarn and backstitch, work in a wheel-like pattern with approx 8 spokes.
Next join the bottom of the spokes together to form a grid.
Continue working down the body working vertical and horizontal backstitches.
Work grid pattern on arms and red part of legs and feet.

THE K FACTOR
THE ACTION FROM ROUND 4

WHO'S GOING THROUGH FROM LAST WEEK?

The knitted item from last week who is going through to the Not Live Final is…
Harry Hill Meerkat!
The rest of you, get knotted!

This week on The K Factor… it's been a slow morning, with Knitted Tiger Woods up first.

WHAT I DID IS NOT ACCEPTABLE. I AM THE ONLY PERSON TO BLAME.

Next up are newlyweds, Bryan and Caroline.

WE WERE ONLY MARRIED YESTERDAY.

SHE'S WITH ME NOW, BRYAN.

In a dramatic twist, Knitted Simon tells Caroline that she should go it alone and leave Bryan.

68

Bessie the Dachshund is up next, and receives a unanimous "yes" from the judges.

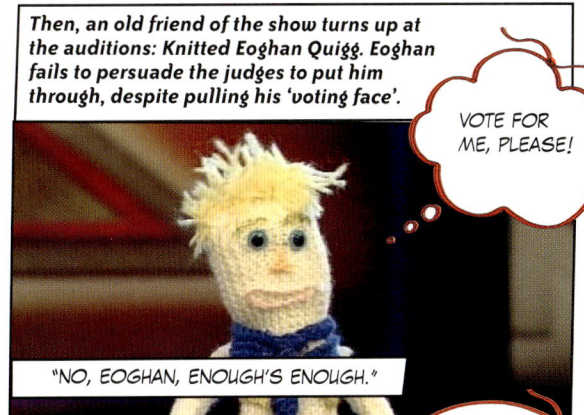

Then, an old friend of the show turns up at the auditions: Knitted Eoghan Quigg. Eoghan fails to persuade the judges to put him through, despite pulling his 'voting face'.

> VOTE FOR ME, PLEASE!

"NO, EOGHAN, ENOUGH'S ENOUGH."

BRYAN'S REVENGE

"MR COWELL'S CONDITION IS STABLE, BUT HE URGENTLY NEEDS A REPAIR."

> YOU'VE RUINED MY LIFE!

During the afternoon session, tragedy strikes, as jilted lover Bryan returns with a pair of scissors.

Before the other judges can stop him, he cuts off Knitted Simon's head.

Knitted Simon's surgeon makes an urgent televised appeal for anyone with some pink wool to come to the hospital immediately. Peter the Duck arrives to help save Simon.

Unfortunately, Knitted Simon's head is sewn on back-to-front.

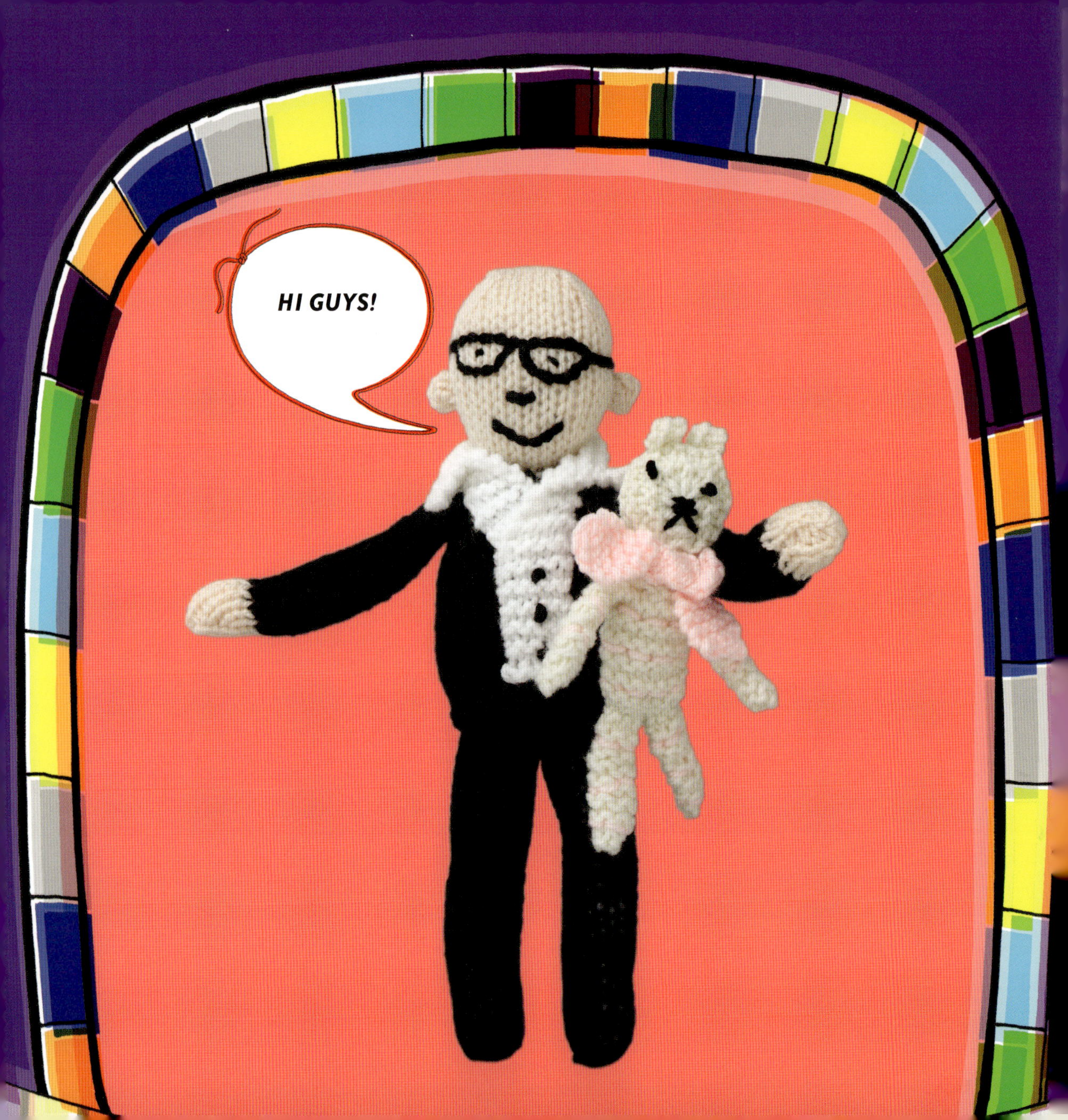
HI GUYS!

THE REAL KNITTED HARRY HILL

MATERIALS

Knitted Harry Hill
Patons Fab DK, approx 68m/25g ball (100% acrylic)
    1 ball in White 2306
    1 ball in Black 2311
Sirdar Bonus DK, approx 280m/100g ball (100% acrylic)
    1 ball in Flesh 963
Pair of 3.75mm needles

Knitted Character
Patons Fab DK, approx 274m/100g ball (100% acrylic)
    1 ball in Cream 2307
    1 ball in Pink 2304
Patons Fab DK, approx 68m/25g ball (100% acrylic)
    1 ball in Black 2311
Pair of 3.75mm needles

The Real Knitted Harry Hill made a surprise visit to The K Factor studios during Knitted Harry Hill Week, to the delight of the many knitted Harrys who auditioned that week. Taking time out from his TV Burp, he popped backstage to meet the contestants and give them some words of advice and encouragement before their auditions.

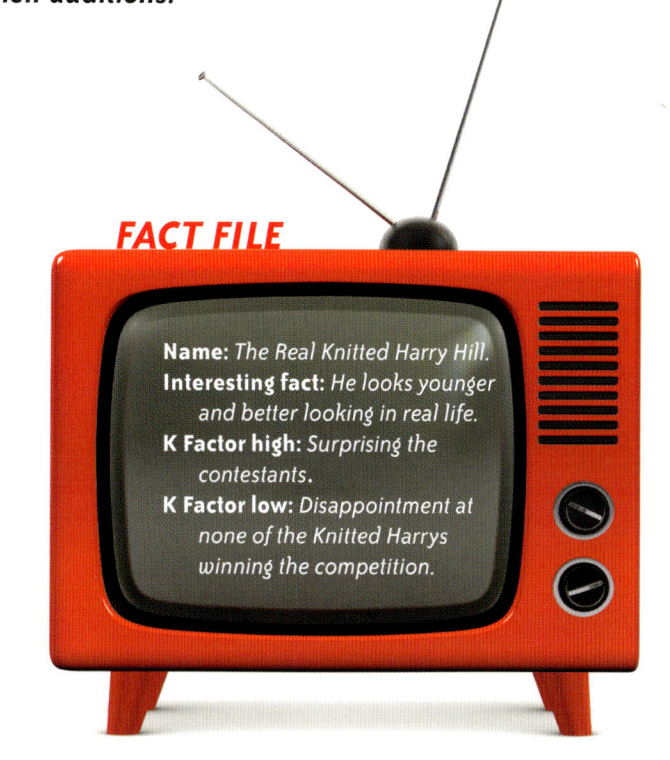

FACT FILE

Name: *The Real Knitted Harry Hill.*
Interesting fact: *He looks younger and better looking in real life.*
K Factor high: *Surprising the contestants.*
K Factor low: *Disappointment at none of the Knitted Harrys winning the competition.*

THE REAL KNITTED HARRY HILL

TENSION
23 stitches and 32 rows over 10cm stocking stitch.

BODY AND HEAD
Work as given for Ninja Clown (p48) using black for body and flesh for head.

LEGS (MAKE 2)
Using 3.75mm needles and black yarn, cast on 14 sts.
Work 30 rows in stocking stitch.
Cast off.
Sew up side and bottom seams, insert stuffing and sew up top seam.

ARMS (MAKE 2)
Worked from top down.
Using 3.75mm needles and black yarn, cast on 11 sts.
Work 24 rows in stocking stitch.
Break off black and join in flesh.
Work 4 rows stocking stitch.
Next row: k1, k2togtbl, knit to last 3 sts, k2tog, k1. (9 sts)
Next row: Purl
Repeat last 2 rows once more. (7 sts)
Break off yarn, thread through sts on needle and pull tight, secure yarn and sew up side seam.
Using picture as guide, attach legs and arms to body.

COLLAR AND SHIRT FRONT
Using 3.75mm needles and white yarn, cast on 5 sts.
Work 18 rows in knit.
Break off yarn and slip onto spare needle.
Repeat from * but do not break off yarn.
Knit across 5 sts on 1st needle, cast on 12 sts, knit across 5 sts on second needle. (22 sts)
Work across all sts.
Starting with a knit row, work a further 6 rows in stocking stitch.
Work 1st collar point as follows.
Next row: K9, turn, sl1, purl to end, turn.
Next row: K5, turn, sl1, purl to end.
Next row: K3, turn, sl1, purl to end.
Knit across all sts.
Repeat for 2nd collar point as given above, changing all the knits to purls and all the purls to knits. Cast off knitwise.
Fold collar on row 4. Using picture as guide, stitch collar and shirt front onto body. Work 3 French knots in black for shirt buttons.

EARS (MAKE 2)
Using 3.75mm needles and flesh yarn, cast on 6 sts.
Row 1: Knit.
Break off yarn and thread through sts on needle.
Pull tight to form a semi-circle shape and secure.
Using picture as guide, attach to head with the cast-on edge to the outside.

FACE
Using picture as guide, embroider face.
Eyes: Black. French knot.
Mouth: Black. Chain stitch.
Nose: Black. Chain stitch.
Glasses: Black. Chain stitch.

SMALL KNITTED CHARACTER

TENSION
23 stitches and 32 rows over 10cm stocking stitch.

BODY
Using 3.75mm needles and cream yarn, cast on 14 sts.
Starting with a knit row, work 12 rows knit.
Row 13: K1, * k2tog, rep from * to last st, k1. (8 sts)
Break off yarn and thread through sts on needle, pull tight and secure; sew down side seam.
Insert a small amount of stuffing.
Sew up bottom seam.

HEAD
Using 3.75mm needles and cream yarn, cast on 8 sts.
Row 1: Knit.
Row 2: K1, * m1, k1, rep from * to end. (15 sts)
Row 3: Knit.
Row 4: * K2, m1, rep from * to last st, k1. (22 sts)
Row 5: Knit.
Row 6: Knit.
Row 7: K1, * k2tog, k1, rep from * to end. (15 sts)
Row 8: Knit.
Row 9: K1, * k2tog, rep from * to end. (8 sts)
Break off yarn and thread through sts on needle and pull tight.
Sew up side seam and attach to body.

LEGS (MAKE 2)
Using 3.75mm needles, cast on 6 sts.
Work 13 rows knit.
Cast off.
Fold in half, sew up top, side and bottom seam.
Attach to bottom of body.

ARMS (MAKE 2)
Using 3.75mm needles cast on 5 sts.
Work 12 rows knit.
Cast off.
Fold in half, sew up top, side and bottom seam.

EARS (MAKE 2)
Cast on 5 sts, cast off 5sts.
Fold ears in half and sew into position on head.

FACE
Using picture as guide, embroider face.
Eyes: Black. French knot.
Nose: Black. Satin stitch.
Mouth: Black. Back stitch.

SCARF
Using 3.75mm needles and pink yarn, cast on 5 sts.
Work every row knit until scarf measures approx 10cm.
Cast off.

STRIPES
Make stripes on body by working backstitch in pink around the body, legs and arms.
Tie scarf around neck.

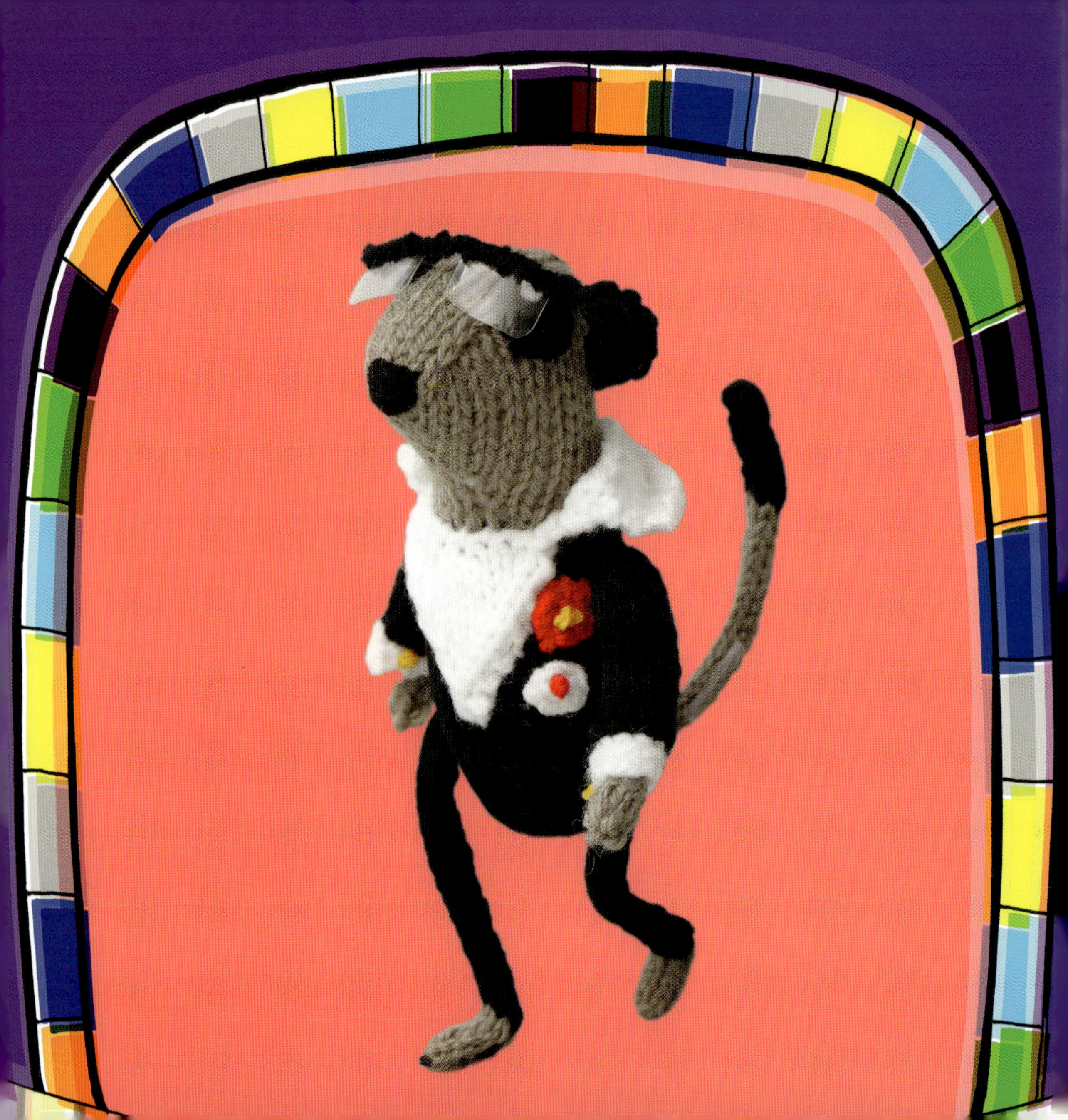

HARRY HILL MEERKAT
FINALIST

Harry Hill Meerkat auditioned during Knitted Harry Hill Week on The K Factor. A popular contestant on the show, the little meerkat was voted through to the Not Live Final – The K Factor on Ice, where he was teamed with Tommy Trundle the elephant. Despite performing some nifty moves on the ice, and wearing a daring canary yellow skating dress, Harry Hill Meerkat did not win the competition.

MATERIALS
Sirdar Country Style DK, approx 318m/100g ball (45% acrylic, 40% nylon, 15% wool)
- 1 ball in Moss Stone 586
- 1 ball in Hopsack 597

Patons Fab DK, approx 68m/25g ball (100% acrylic)
- 1 ball in Black 2311
- 1 ball in White 2306
- Oddments in yellow and red

Pair of 3.75mm straight needles and two double-pointed needles.

Three black pipe cleaners
Clear plastic from bottle

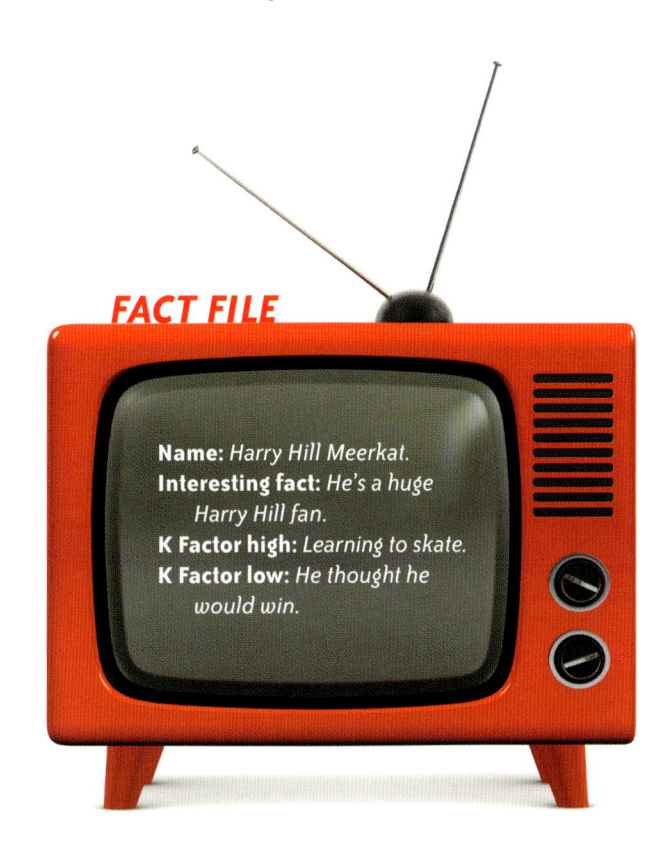

FACT FILE
Name: Harry Hill Meerkat.
Interesting fact: He's a huge Harry Hill fan.
K Factor high: Learning to skate.
K Factor low: He thought he would win.

TENSION
23 stitches and 32 rows over 10cm stocking stitch.

BODY AND HEAD
Using 3.75mm needles and black yarn, cast on 16 sts.
Row 1 (WS): Purl.
Row 2 (RS): K3, m1, k1, m1, k8, m1, k1, m1, k3. (20 sts)
Row 3: Purl.
Row 4: K4, m1, k1, m1, k10, m1, k1, m1, k4. (24 sts)
Starting with a purl row, work 17 rows stocking stitch.
Row 22: K2, * k2tog, k1, rep from * to last st, k1. (17 sts)
Break off black, join in moss stone.
Row 23: Purl.
Row 24: K8, m1, k1, m1, k8. (19 sts)
Row 25: Purl.
Row 26: K9, m1, k1, m1, k9. (21 sts)
Row 27: Purl.
Row 28: K10, m1, k1, m1, k10. (23 sts)
Row 29: Purl.
Row 30: K11, m1, k1, m1, k11. (25 sts)
Row 31: Purl.
Row 32: K12, m1, k1, m1, k12. (27 sts)
Row 33: Purl.
Shape top as follows.
K15, k2togtbl, turn, *Sl1, p3, p2tog, turn, sl1, k3, k2togtbl, turn, rep from * until all stitches on the needles have been worked.
Break off yarn, leaving a good length. Draw through remaining sts on needle and pull tight. Sew up back seam of head and body. Insert stuffing from bottom. Sew up seam.

LEGS (MAKE 2)
Using 3.5mm double-pointed needles and moss stone yarn, make I-cord as follows:
Cast on 5 sts. Do not turn needle, slide sts up to RHS of needle and knit to end. Work a further 4 rows as above. Break off moss stone and join in black. Work a further 25 rows.
Break off yarn and thread through sts on needle.
Insert pipe cleaner down through the centre of I-cord. Cut pipe cleaner to required length. Sew up bottom end to stop pipe cleaner coming out. Bend at foot and bend approx 2.5cm from top, for knee. Using picture as guide, pin and stitch into position on body.

ARMS (MAKE 2)
Using 3.5mm double-pointed needles and moss stone yarn, make I-cord as follows:
Cast on 4 sts, do not turn, slide sts up to RHS of needle and knit to end. Work a further 15 rows.
Break off yarn and thread through sts on needle. Insert pipe cleaner down through the centre of I-cord. Cut pipe cleaner to required length. Sew up bottom end to stop pipe cleaner coming out. Using picture as guide, pin and stitch into position on body.

TAIL
Using 3.5mm double-pointed needles and black yarn, make I-cord as follows:
Cast on 4 sts. Do not turn needle, slide sts up to RHS of needle and knit to end. Work a further 5 rows.
Break off black yarn and join in moss stone. Work a further 20 rows.
Break off yarn and thread through sts on needle.
Insert pipe cleaner down through the centre of I-cord. Cut pipe cleaner to required length. Sew up bottom end to stop pipe cleaner coming out. Using picture as guide, pin and stitch into position onto centre back of body.
.
SLEEVES (MAKE 2)
Using 3.75mm needles and black yarn, cast on 10 sts.
Starting with a knit row, work 10 rows in stocking stitch.
Next row: K1, * K2tog, rep from * to last st, k1.
Break off yarn and thread through sts on needle; secure and sew up side seam. Insert arm into sleeve and stitch together.

CUFFS (MAKE 2)

Using 3.75mm needles, cast on 12 sts, cast off 12 sts.
Fold around arm at base of sleeve, stitch into position, making sure that a couple of stitches overlap to form cuff detail. Work a French knot in yellow for cufflink. Using picture as guide, sew sleeves to body.

SHIRT FRONT

Using 3.75mm needles and white yarn, cast on 11 sts.
Row 1 (WS): K1, p9, k1.
Row 2 (RS): K1, k2togtbl, k2, m1, k1, m1, k2, k2tog, k1.
Row 3: K1, purl to last st, k1.
Row 4: K1, k2togtbl, knit to last 3 sts, k2tog, k1. (7 sts)
Row 5: As row 3.
Row 6: K1, k2togtbl, k1, k2tog, k1. (5 sts)
Row 7: As row 3.
Row 8: K1, sl1, k2tog, psso, k1. (3 sts)
Row 9: K1, p1, k1.
Break off yarn and thread through 3 sts on needle. Pull tight and secure. Using picture as guide, pin and stitch onto centre front of body.

COLLAR

Using 3.75mm needles and white yarn, cast on 17 sts.
Row 1 (WS): K1, purl to last st, k1.
Work 1st collar point as follows using short row shaping technique.
Next row (RS): K7, turn.
Next row: Sl1, purl to last st, k1.
Next row: K5, turn.
Next row: Sl1, purl to last st, k1.
Next row: Knit to end.
Work 2nd collar point as follows.
Next row: K1, p6, turn.
Next row: Sl1, knit to end.
Next row: K1, p4, turn.
Next row: Sl1, knit to end.
Next row: K1, purl to last st, k1.
Repeat the last row twice more.
Next row: Knit to end.
Next row: K1, purl to last st, k1.
Cast off. Sew in loose ends, using picture as guide; fold collar over and stitch into position.

EYES (MAKE 2)

Using 3.25mm needles and black yarn cast on 10 sts.
Row 1: Knit to end.
Row 2: * P2tog, rep from * to end. (5 sts)
Thread yarn through sts on needle and pull tight; sew up sides to form circle. Place on head and stitch into position. Work 1 French knot in white to finish off yarn.

EARS (MAKE 2)

Using 3.25mm needles, cast on 8 sts.
Row 1: Knit to end.
Row 2: Knit to end.
Thread through sts on needle; pull tight.
Place the edge that the stitches have been pulled at onto head and stitch into position.

BADGE (MAKE 2)

Using 3.25mm needles and red yarn, cast on 6 sts.
Row 1: Knit to end.
Thread through sts on needle and pull tight; sew up sides to form circle. Sew side seams together to form circle. Work white badge as red, but cast on 3 sts instead of 6. Stitch the badges into position on body. Work French knots at the centres to add detail.

GLASSES

Cut 2 pieces of plastic approx 2.5cm wide and 1.5cm deep from a clean plastic bottle. Round off the bottom edge of the plastic pieces.
Using a sharp sewing needle, pierce 3 holes along top edge of plastic lenses. Cut a pipe cleaner to approx 12cm, fold back at each end to form the arms. Split the black yarn into 2 strands; thread sharp needle, and using an over stitch, secure lenses to the frame. Place the glasses onto head and sew into position around the arms.

FACE

Using picture as guide, embroider face.
Nose: Black. Satin stitch.

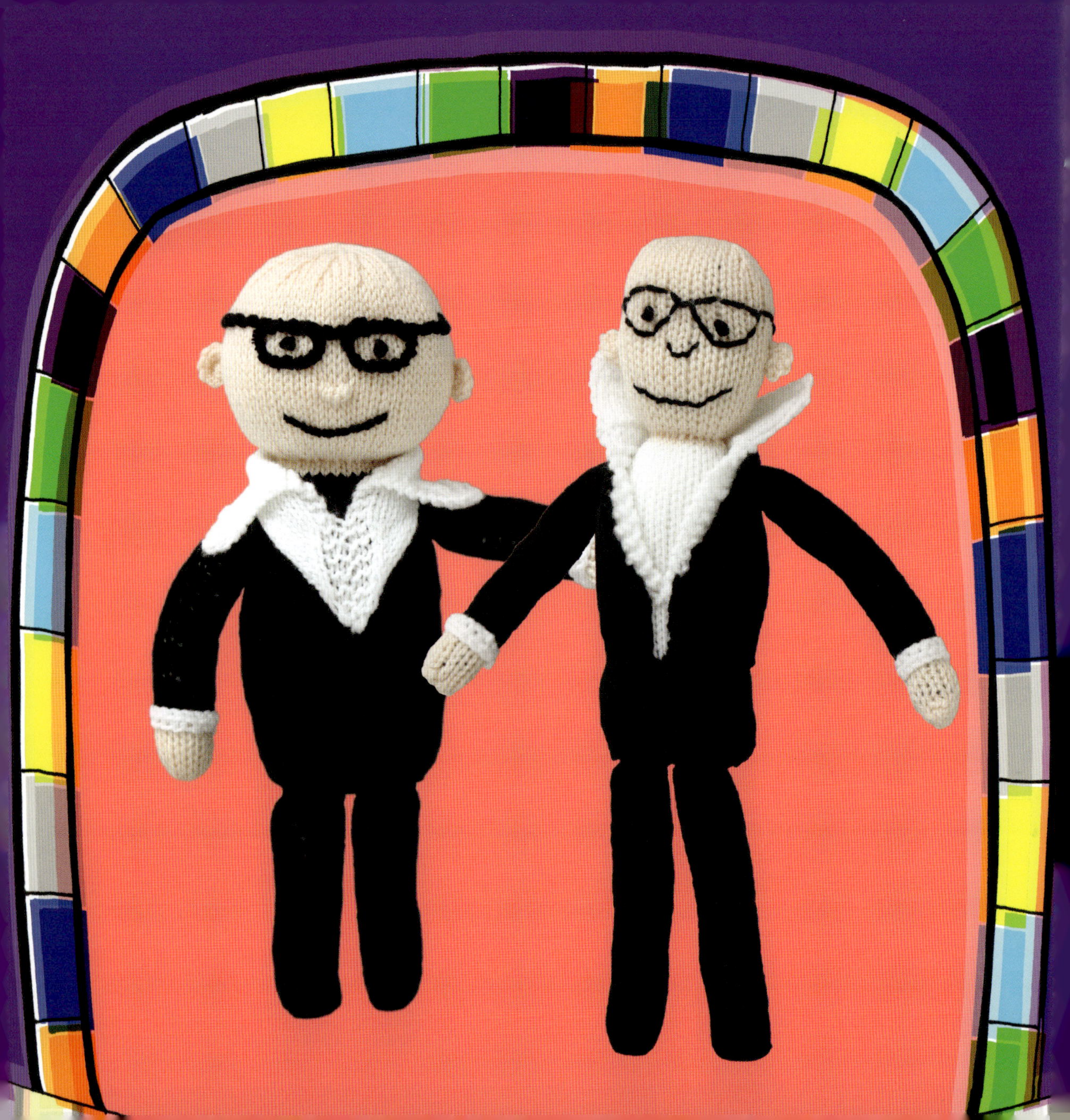

KNITTED HARRY HILLS

MATERIALS

Knitted Harry Hill 1
Sirdar Bonus DK, approx 280m/100g ball (100% acrylic)
    1 ball in Flesh 963
Patons Fab DK, approx 68m/25g ball (100% acrylic)
    1 ball in White 2306
    1 ball in Black 2311
Pair of 3.75mm needles

One black pipe cleaner

Knitted Harry Hill 2
Sirdar Bonus DK, approx 280m/100g ball (100% acrylic)
    1 ball in Flesh 963
Patons Fab DK, approx 68m/25g ball (100% acrylic)
    1 ball in White 2306
    1 ball in Black 2311
Pair of 3.75mm needles

During Knitted Harry Hill Week on The K Factor, the contestants were asked to dress up as Harry Hill. An impressive array of Harrys auditioned in front of the judges, all with a slightly different take on Harry's distinctive style. While a few of the Knitted Harrys stood out from the crowd, many of them ultimately failed to impress the judging panel.

FACT FILE

Name: Knitted Harry Hill 1, Knitted Harry Hill 2.
Interesting fact: They hadn't met before they applied for the K Factor.
K Factor high: Meeting the Real Knitted Harry Hill.
K Factor low: Not getting through to the Not Live Final.

KNITTED HARRY HILL 1

TENSION
23 stitches and 32 rows over 10cm stocking stitch.

BODY AND HEAD
Work as given for Knitted Simon Cowell (p24).

LEGS
Work as given for Knitted Simon Cowell (p24).

ARMS (MAKE 2)
Worked from top down.
Using 3.75mm needles and black yarn, cast on 14 sts.
Starting with a knit row, work 24 rows stocking stitch.
Break off black yarn and join in flesh.
Work a further 8 rows stocking stitch.
Break off yarn and thread through sts on needle, pull tight and secure.
Sew up side seam.
Insert stuffing and sew up top seam.

CUFFS (MAKE 2)
Using 3.75mm needles and white yarn, cast on 16 sts, then cast off 16 sts.
Stitch into place at bottom of sleeves.
Sew in loose ends.

EARS (MAKE 2)
Using 3.75mm needles and flesh yarn, cast on 7 sts.
Row 1: Knit.
Row 2: Knit.
Break off yarn and thread through sts on needle.
Pull tight to form a semi-circle shape and secure.
Using picture as guide, attach to head with the cast-on edge to the outside.

COLLAR AND SHIRT FRONT
Using 3.75mm needles and white yarn, cast on 44 sts.
Row 1: Knit.
Row 2: Knit.
Row 3: K2, k2togtbl, knit last 4 sts, k2tog, K2. (42 sts)
Row 4: K2, purl to last 2 sts, K2.
Row 5: K2, k2togtbl, knit last 4 sts, k2tog, k2. (40 sts)
Row 6: K2, p2tog, purl to last 4 sts, p2togtbl, k2. (38 sts)
Repeat rows 5–6 once more then row 5 again. (32 sts)
Row 10: As row 4.
Row 11: As row 1.
Change to reverse stocking stitch.
Row 12: Knit.
Row 13: K2, purl to last 2 sts, k2.
Repeat the last 2 rows 4 more times.
Row 22: Knit.
Row 23: K2, p6, cast off 16 sts, p6, k2.
Work each side separately.
Row 1: Knit.
Row 2: P6, k2.
Repeat last 2 rows twice more.
Row 7: K2, k2togtbl, k4. (7 sts)
Row 8: P5, k2.
Row 9: K2, k2togtbl, k3. (6 sts)
Row 10: P4, k2.
Row 11: K2, k2togtbl, k2. (5 sts)
Row 12: P3, k2.
Row 13: K2, k2togtbl, k1. (4 sts)
Row 14: P2, k2.
Row 15: K2, k2togtbl. (3 sts)

Row 16: P1, k2.
Row 17: Sl2, k1, psso. (1st)
Slip yarn through last st and fasten off.
Break off yarn and rejoin to work other side as follows.
Row 1: Knit.
Row 2: K2, p6.
Repeat last 2 rows twice more.
Row 7: K4, k2tog, k2 .(7 sts)
Row 8: K2, p5.
Row 9: K3, k2tog, k2. (6 sts)
Row 10: K2, p4.
Row 11: K2, k2togtbl, k2. (5 sts)
Row 12: K2, p3.
Row 13: K1, k2tog, k2. (4 sts)
Row 14: K2, p2.
Row 15: K2tog, k2. (3 sts)
Row 16: K2, p1.
Row 17: Sl1, k2tog, psso. (1 st)
Slip yarn through last st and fasten off.
Break off yarn.
Using picture as guide, stitch collar and shirt front onto body.

FACE

Using picture as guide, embroider face.
Eyes: Black. French knot.
Mouth: Black. Chain stitch.
Nose: Make by pinching together small section of face and working a few stitches with flesh yarn to secure shape.

GLASSES

Take black pipe cleaner and, at approx halfway point, create a loop; repeat this so you have 2 circles in the centre. Make sure both circles are the same size.
Place on head, using picture as guide. Stitch into place.

KNITTED HARRY HILL 2

TENSION

23 stitches and 32 rows over 10cm stocking stitch.

BODY AND HEAD

Work as given for Knitted Rolando (p34), using black for body and flesh for head.

LEGS (MAKE 2)

Work as given for Knitted Rolando (p34) in black and flesh.

ARMS (MAKE 2)

Work as given for Knitted Rolando (p34) in black and flesh.

JACKET

Using 3.75mm needle and black yarn, cast on 36 sts.
Starting with a knit row, work 8 rows in stocking stitch.
Row 9: K1, k2togtbl, k to last 3 sts, k2tog, k1. (34 sts)
Row 10: Purl.
Row 11: Knit.
Row 12: Purl.
Repeat last 4 rows twice more. (30 sts)
Row 21: K1, k2togtbl, k1, k2tog, k2, k2togtbl, k10, k2tog, k2, k2togtbl, k1, k2tog, k1. (24 sts)
Row 22: Purl.
Row 23: K2, k2tog, k2, k2togtbl, k8, k2tog, k2, k2togtbl, k2. (20 sts)
Row 24: Purl.
Row 25: Knit.
Cast off knitwise.

COLLAR AND SHIRT FRONT

*Using 3.75mm needles and white yarn, cast on 5 sts.
Work 20 rows in knit.
Break off yarn and slip onto spare needle.
Repeat from * but do not break off yarn.
Knit across 5 sts on 1st needle, cast on 12 sts, knit across 5 sts on second needle (22 sts).
Work across all sts.
Starting with a knit row, work a further 6 rows stocking stitch.
Work 1st collar point as follows.
Next row: K9, turn, sl1, purl to end, turn.
Next row: K5, turn, sl1, purl to end.
Next row: K3, turn, sl1, purl to end.
Knit across all sts.
Repeat for 2nd collar point as given above, changing all the knits to purls and all the purls to knits.
Cast off knitwise.
Fold collar on row 4.
Using picture as guide, stitch collar and shirt front onto body.
Pin jacket to body and stitch into place.
Stitch arms to jacket using shaping marks as guide.

CUFFS (MAKE 2)

Using 3.75mm needles and white yarn, cast on 14 sts, then cast off 14 sts.
Stitch into place at bottom of sleeves.
Sew in loose ends.

EARS (MAKE 2)

Using 3.75mm needles and flesh yarn, cast on 6 sts.
Row 1: Knit.
Break off yarn and thread through sts on needle.
Pull tight to form a semi-circle shape and secure.
Using picture as guide, attach to head with the cast-on edge to the outside.

FACE

Using picture as guide, embroider face.
Eyes: Black. French knot.
Mouth: Black. Backstitch.
Nose: Black. Backstitch.
Glasses: Black. Backstitch.

KNITTED HARRY HILL WEEK

For Round 3 of The K Factor, contestants were invited to dress up as Harry Hill. It was a great success, with entrants from all over the country. The Real Knitted Harry Hill surprised the contestants by taking time out of TV Burp to visit the set.

THE K FACTOR
THE ACTION FROM ROUND 5

WHO'S GOING THROUGH FROM LAST WEEK?

The knitted item from last week who is safe and going through to the Not Live Final is…
Bessie the Dachshund!
The rest of you, get knotted!

It's Bird Week on The K Factor, and birds from all over Britain have converged on the K Factor studios.

"LUMPY AND TEDIOUS. IT'S A 'NO'".

But, with only one week to go before the Not Live Final, there's growing anger about Peter the Duck's absence from the line-up after being barred from entry in Round 1 due to not having any wings. A group of Peter's supporters stage a protest outside studios, which soon gets nasty.

YOU ARE GOING TO LEAVE HERE, PETER, WITH NOTHING.

To cheer himself up, Peter has entered himself into Michael Winner's Dining Stars, but fails to win over Michael Winner.

Feelings of failure well up inside the tiny duck, and he's determined to end it all. While plummeting from a cliff, Knitted Simon catches him.

"I LOVE YOU PETER!"

YOU DIDN'T THINK I'D TURN MY BACK ON YOU AFTER YOU SAVED MY LIFE, DID YOU? YOU'RE THROUGH!

WE WERE ONLY MARRIED YESTERDAY.

BRYAN AND CAROLINE

Newlyweds Bryan and Caroline were at the centre of a dramatic day during The K Factor auditions. Knitted Simon Cowell told Caroline that he didn't like Bryan, and that she should go it alone. Caroline wasted no time in following his advice, ditching her new husband and leaving with Simon. Jilted lover Bryan was to return later that day, telling Simon, "You've ruined my life", and cutting off his head with a pair of scissors. Caroline did not make it through to the Not Live Final, and divorced Bryan soon after the show.

MATERIALS
Caroline
Patons Fab DK, approx 274m/100g ball
(100% acrylic)
    1 ball in White 2306
Patons Fab DK, approx 68m/25g ball
(100% acrylic)
    1 ball in Black 2311
    1 ball in Cherry 2322
    1 ball in Brown 2309
    1 ball in Forest 2319
Sirdar Bonus DK, approx 280m/100g ball
(100% acrylic)
    1 ball in Flesh 963
Pair of 3.75mm needles

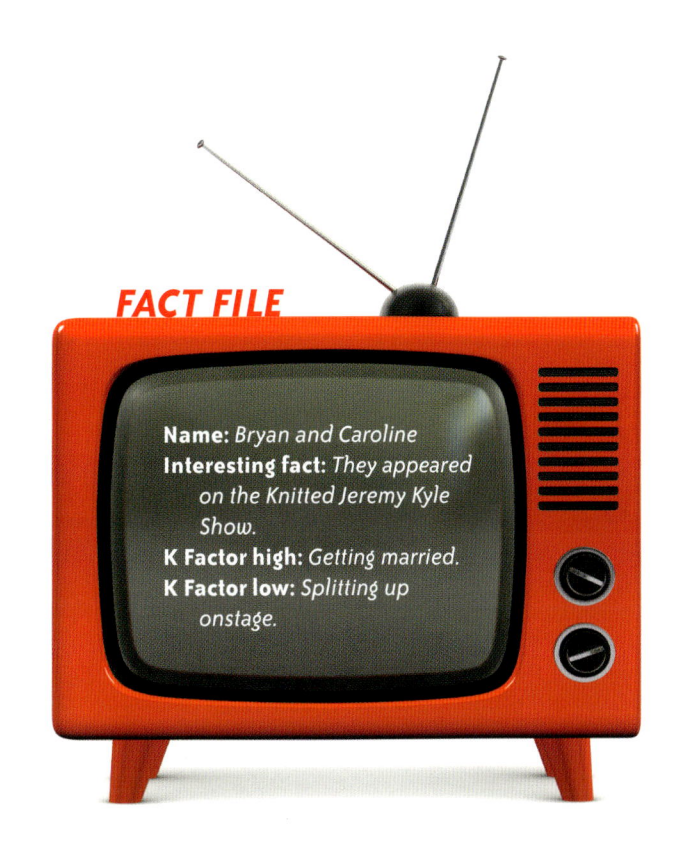

FACT FILE
Name: Bryan and Caroline
Interesting fact: They appeared on the Knitted Jeremy Kyle Show.
K Factor high: Getting married.
K Factor low: Splitting up onstage.

CAROLINE

TENSION
23 stitches and 32 rows over 10cm stocking stitch.

BODY AND HEAD
Work as given for Ninja Clown (p48) in white and flesh.

LEGS (MAKE 2)
Work as given for Ninja Clown (p48), but work rows 1–8 in white, before breaking off white yarn and joining in flesh for remaining rows.

ARMS (MAKE 2)
Work as given for Ninja Clown (p48) in white and flesh.

SKIRT
Worked from the top down.
Using 3.75mm needles and white yarn, cast on 27 sts.
Work 5 rows knit.
Row 6: Purl.
Row 7: K1, * m1, k1, rep from * to end. (53 sts)
Starting with a purl row, work in stocking stitch for 25 rows.
Row 32 (WS): Knit.
Row 33 (RS): K1, * k2togtbl, yfwd, rep from * to last 2sts, k2.
Row 34: Knit.
Row 35: Knit.
Row 36: Purl.
Row 37: Knit.
Repeat the last 6 rows once more, then rows 32–34 once more.
Starting and ending with a knit row, work in stocking stitch for 6 rows.
Next row: As row 33.
Work a further 3 rows in stocking stitch.
Cast off.
Sew up back seam of skirt. Fold bottom hem over at last lace row to form picot edge.
Stitch hem into place.
Slip skirt onto body and stitch into place.

VEIL
Using white yarn and 4mm needles, cast on 18 sts using lace cast-on method.
Row 1: Knit.
Row 2: * Knit into next stitch by wrapping the yarn round the needle twice, rep from * to 4 sts, k4.
Repeat the last 2 rows a further 14 times.
Row 31: Knit to end.
Cast off loosely.
Thread yarn through narrow end of veil and pull tight into a circle.

HAIR
Using 3.75mm needles and brown yarn, cast on 12 sts.
Rows 1–3 : Knit.
Row 4: K8, turn.
Row 5: Sl1, knit to end.
Row 6: K4, turn.
Row 7: Sl1, knit to end.
Row 8: K8, turn.
Row 9: Sl1, knit to end.
Rows 10–13: Knit.
Row 14: k1, k2tog, knit to end. (11 sts)
Row 15: K to last 3 sts, k2tog, k1. (10 sts)
Row 16: Cast off 4 sts, knit to end. (6 sts)
Rows 17–22: Knit.
Row 23: K6, cast on 4 sts. (10 sts)
Row 24: Knit.
Row 25: Knit to last st, m1, k1. (11 sts)
Row 26: K1, m1, knit to end. (12 sts)
Rows 27–29: Knit.
Rows 30: As row 4.
Row 31: As row 5.
Row32: As row 6.
Row 33: As row 7.
Row 34: As row 8.
Row 35: As row 9.
Rows 36–37: Knit.
Cast off.
Sew up back seam;

and sew up top seam.
Sew in all loose ends.
Using picture as guide, fit hair onto head.
Pin into position and stitch into place on head.
Stitch veil into position on top of head.

CUFFS (MAKE 2)
Using 3.75mm needles and white yarn, cast on 14 sts, then cast off 14 sts.
Pin into position at the bottom of white sleeve. Stitch onto arms.

COLLAR
Using 3.75mm needles and white yarn, cast on 35 sts; then cast off 35 sts.
Pin into position at dress neckline. Stitch to body.

FLOWERS (MAKE 5)
Using 3.75mm needles, cast on 16 sts.
Row 1: K1, *cast off the next 2 sts, do not use the last stitch on the RH needle as part of the next repeat, rep from * to end. (6 sts)
Break off yarn, leave a long enough length for sewing up; pull through sts on needle.

Let the flower roll up on itself then stitch into shape.

LEAVES (MAKE 3)
Using 3.75mm needles and green yarn, cast on 8 sts.
Row 1: K6, turn.
Row 2: Sl1, knit to end.
Row 3: K4, turn.
Row 4: Sl1, Knit to end.
Row 5: Knit across all sts on needle. Cast off.
Break off leaving good length for sewing up and forming flower stalk.
Using loose end of yarn, thread through the flat edge of leaf and pull tight to form a cupped shape.

BOUQUET
Sew 2 flowers on to cupped edge of 2 leaves, then 1 flower onto last leaf.
Sew in tail ends of flowers.
Tie the green tails from leaves together to form bouquet. Trim green tails to form stalks.

FACE
Using picture as guide, embroider face.
Eyes: Black.
Mouth: Cherry.

BRYAN

MATERIALS
Bryan
Patons Diploma Gold DK, approx 125m/50g ball (55% wool, 45% acrylic)
    1 ball in Steel 6184
Patons Fab DK, approx 68m/25g ball (100% acrylic)
    1 ball in Black 2311
    1 ball in Cherry 2322
    1 ball in Brown 2309
    1 ball in White 2306
    1 ball in Yellow 2305
Sirdar Bonus DK, approx 280m/100g ball (100% acrylic)
    1 ball in Flesh 963
Sirdar Country Style DK, approx 318m/100g ball (45% acrylic, 40% nylon, 15% wool)
    1 ball in Gemini 502
Pair of 3.75mm needles

TENSION
23 stitches and 32 rows over 10cm stocking stitch.

BODY AND HEAD
Work as given for Ninja Clown (p48) in steel and flesh.

LEGS (MAKE 2)
Work as given for Ninja Clown (p48), but work rows 1-8 in black, before breaking off black yarn and joining in steel for remaining rows.

ARMS (MAKE 2)
Work as given for Ninja Clown (p48) in steel and flesh, but do not sew arms onto body yet – these will be attached to the coat.

JACKET
Work each side of tail separately
Left-hand tail
Using 3.75mm needles and steel yarn, cast on 3 sts.
Row 1 (WS): Knit.
Row 2 (RS): K1, m1, k2. (4 sts)
Row 3: Knit.
Row 4: K2, m1, k2. (5 sts)
Row 5: Knit.
Row 6: K3, m1, k2. (6 sts)
Row 7: K2, p2, k2.
Row 8: K4, m1, k2. (7 sts)
Row 9: K2, p3, k2.
Row 10: K5, m1, k2. (8 sts)
Row 11: K2, p4, k2.
Row 12: K6, m1, k2. (9 sts)
Row 13: K2, p5, k2.
Row 14: K7, m1, k2. (10 sts)
Row 15: K2, p6, k2.
Slip sts on to stitch holder.
Right-hand tail
Using 3.75mm needles and steel yarn, cast on 3 sts.
Row 1 (WS): Knit.
Row 2 (RS): K2, m1, k1. (4 sts)
Row 3: Knit.
Row 4: K2, m1, k2. (5 sts)
Row 5: Knit.
Row 6: K2, m1, k3. (6 sts)
Row 7: K2, p2, k2.
Row 8: K2, m1, k4. (7 sts)
Row 9: K2, p3, k2.
Row 10: K2, m1, k5. (8 sts)
Row 11: K2, p4, k2.
Row 12: K2, m1, k6. (9 sts)
Row 13: K2, p5, k2.
Row 14: K2, m1, k7. (10 sts)
Row 15: K2, p6, k2.
Join tails together, with increases edges to the outside work as follows.
Row 16: Right-hand tail, k2, m1, k8; left-hand tail, k8, m1, K2. (22 sts)
Row 17: K2, p7, (k2tog) twice, p7, k2. (20 sts)
Row 18: K2, m1, k16, m1, k2. (22 sts)
Row 19: K2, p18, k2.
Row 20: K2, m1, k18, m1, k2. (24 sts)
Row 21: K2, p20, k2.
Row 22: K2, m1, k20, m1, k2. (26 sts)
Row 23: K2, p22, k2.
Row 24: K2, m1, k22, m1, k2. (28 sts)
Row 25: K2, p24, k2.
Row 26: K2, m1, k24, m1, k2. (30 sts)
Row 27: K2, p26, k2.
Row 28: K2, m1, k28, m1, k2. (32 sts)
Row 29: K2, p28, k2.
Row 30: Cast on 2 sts at the beg of row, and then knit to end. (34 sts)
Row 31: Cast on 2 sts at the beg of row, and then k4, p28, K4. (36 sts)
Row 32: Knit to end.
Row 33: K4, p28, K4.
Repeat last 2 rows twice more.
Row 38: K7, k2tog, k2, k2togtbl, k10, k2tog, k2, k2togtbl, k7. (32 sts)
Row 39: K4, p24, k4.
Row 40: K6, k2tog, k2, k2togtbl, k8, k2tog, k2, k2togtbl, k6. (28 sts)
Row 41: K4, p20, k4.
Rows 42-44: Knit.
Cast off.

COLLAR
Using 3.75mm needles and white yarn, cast on 22 sts.
Row 1: Knit
Row 2: Purl.
Row 3: Knit.
Row 4: Knit.
Work rest of collar as follows.
Next row: K6, turn, Sl1, p5 to end.
Next row: Knit to end.
Next row: P6, turn, Sl1, k5 to end.
Cast off knitwise.

Fold collar over at row 4, stitch into place around neck.
Stitch jacket into place – using picture as guide.
Stitch arms into place – use shaping marks on jacket as guide.

CRAVAT

Using 3.75mm needles and gemini yarn, cast on 7 sts.
Starting with a purl row, work in stocking stitch for 5 rows.
Row 6: K1, k2togtbl, k1, k2tog, k1. (5 sts)
Row 7: Purl.
Row 8: K1, Sl1, k2tog, psso, k1. (3 sts)
Row 9: P3tog.
Break off yarn and pull through sts on needle. Pull tight.
Sew in loose ends.
Stitch into position on body between collars.
Add a horizontal straight stitch and a French knot in yellow as tie pin if desired.

TOP HAT

Using 3.75mm needles and black yarn, cast on 10 sts.
Row 1 (WS): Purl.
Row 2 (RS): K2, * m1, k1, rep from * to end. (18 sts)
Row 3: Purl.
Row 4: K3, m1,* k2, m1, rep from * to last st, k1. (26 sts)
Row 5: Purl.
Row 6: K4, m1,* k3, m1, rep from * to last st, k1. (34 sts)
Row 7: Knit.
Starting with a knit row, work a further 10 rows in stocking stitch.
Row 18: Knit.
Row 19: K5, m1,* k4, m1, rep from * to last st, k1. (42 sts)
Row 20: Purl.
Row 21: K6, m1,* k5, m1, rep from * to last st, k1. (50 sts)
Cast off knitwise.
Sew up top, side and brim seams.
Sew in loose ends.
Cut a circle of cardboard to fit the top of the hat and a strip of cardboard the depth of the hat. Push the circle of cardboard into the hat then roll the strip up and ease into the hat. Secure with a small piece of tape.

HAIR

Make as Caroline – place on head and stitch into place.
Place hat on head and stitch into place.

WAISTCOAT

Using picture as guide, work Swiss darning technique; embroider 1 line up the centre of body on every stitch, starting approx 6 rows up.
Use graph (right) as guide to work right and left sides of waistcoat.

FLOWER

Using 3.75mm needles and cherry yarn, work 1 flower as given for Caroline's flowers.

FACE

Using picture as guide, embroider face.
Eyes: Black – as French knot, wrapped around needle approx 5 times.
Mouth: Black. Backstitch.

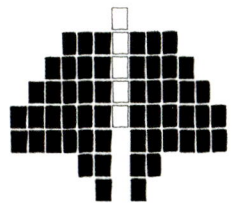

THE K FACTOR
THE ACTION FROM THE NOT LIVE FINAL – THE K FACTOR ON ICE

It's the Not Live Final, and this week the format is slightly different: it's The K Factor on Ice.

Knitted Phillip Schofield and Knitted Holly Willoughby welcome the skating stars onto the ice...

Winston Stimson... Tommy Trundle... Harry Hill Meerkat... Bessie the Dachshund... and Peter the Duck.

The finalists have been put in pairs and taught how to skate, but because there are only five of them, Peter is forced to skate by himself.

> I CAN'T LET DOWN THE FANS. I WILL BE SKATING.

At the dress rehearsal, tragedy strikes. Winston falls awkwardly and injures his leg. Sadly, the leg is broken, although Winston vows to carry on.

First onto the ice is Peter the Duck.

Knitted Torville and Dean...

"PETER, THAT WAS A MESS - AND WHERE ARE YOUR WINGS?"

"PETER'S FINDING IT QUITE HARD. WITH NO WINGS, BALANCE IS A PROBLEM FOR HIM."

Next on are Tommy Trundle and Harry Hill Meerkat.

In a very ambitious move, Winston Stimson and Bessie decide to change their song at the last minute to Ravel's "Bolero". Will Winston be able to do that lift?

"THEY'RE ALL FINDING IT DIFFICULT MOVING AROUND ON ICE, BECAUSE IT'S SO SLIPPY."

CROCHET CONFESSION!

THE KNITTED CHARACTER COMES CLEAN...

"HARRY, I'VE GOT A CONFESSION TO MAKE. THE FACT IS, I'M NOT KNITTED. I'M CROCHETED!"

THEN YOU MEAN THE ENTIRE K FACTOR: SO YOU THINK YOU CAN KNIT? HAS BEEN BUILT ON A LIE?

I'M AFRAID SO.

All the contestants are back in the studio ready to hear Harry announce the winner. But first, a song...

DON'T STOP BELIEVIN'...!

AND THE WINNER IS...

The finalists gather round to hear the result. And the Winner of The K Factor is...

...Peter the Duck!!

And to accept the coveted K Factor trophy, the person who brought him into the world – it's Andy!

PUBLISHER'S ACKNOWLEDGEMENTS

This book would not have happened without the initial encouragement of a big K Factor fan and champion Barbara Dixon. Thanks also to Nina Sharman for first picking up the phone to Avalon and getting the ball rolling and James Taylor, Alice Russell and the team at Avalon Management for agreeing to allow us to turn a fabulous TV slot into a book. Julia Halford, Amy Christian, Laura Russell, Luise Roberts, Morna McPherson and Gemma Wilson have all played vital roles in turning this into a great book, and special thanks to Holly Jolliffe, who took the fantastic photographs and Laura Stimpson who produced the illustrations.

Most of all thanks to all of the members of the public who submitted their knitting projects to The K Factor and to the hugely talented Carol Meldrum for painstakingly recreating and adapting these projects and patterns for publication on a horrendously tight schedule through a very snowy Christmas – Carol you are an absolute star! Carol would like to thank her other half, Andy Daly, for all his patience and support!

Original projects created by:
Knitted Simon Cowell and Knitted Cheryl Cole – Jane Burns; Knitted Rolando Off Popstar to Operastar – Hillary Sleiman; Peter the Duck – Andy Hunt; Winston Stimson – Linda Stimson; Ninja Clown – Mrs Parsons; Philnut – Margaret Smith; Gary – Maddie Newman; Knitted Spider-Man – Carol Allen; The Real Knitted Harry Hill – Mrs P Hinett; Harry Hill Meerkat – Heather Leavers; Bryan and Caroline – Bryan and Caroline Fermore.

With thanks to all the other knitters who contributed projects, including: Jane Burns, Catherine Cann, Christine Carl, Martine Cooper, Sarah Cox, Lucinda Dav, Ali Davies, Emily Day, Amie Drummond, Ky Elkins, Sylvia Flint, Andrew Greetham, Emma Haggan, Abigail Hartshorne, Andi Hopwood, Jayne Howell, Keith Jimpson, Jan Lockwood, Fred Munton & Glynis Campbell, Zoe Oliver, Amy Paisey, Mrs C Robertson, Lorraine Robertson, Shelia Rushbury, Holly Searle, Hillary Sleiman, Catherine Tennick. The publishers have made all reasonable efforts to include acknowledgment of all knitting contributors to the K Factor represented in the book.

Finally, our biggest thanks to Harry Hill for The K Factor.

Techniques and Abbreviations

approx	approximately
alt	alternate
beg	beginning
ch	chain
cm	centimetre
dc	double chain
dc2tog	double crochet two stitches together
dec	decrease
inc	increase
K	knit
K2tog	knit two together
K2togtbl	knit two together through back of the loop
K3tog	knit three together
L1	make one loop stitch
LH	left hand
M1	make one
mm	millimetre(s)
oz	ounce(s)
P	purl
P2tog	purl two together
P2togtbl	purl two together through back of the loop
P3tog	purl three together
rem	remaining
rnd	round
psso	pass slipped stitch over
rep	repeat
RH	right hand
RS	right side
sl	slip
St st	Stocking stitch
st(s)	stitch(es)
tbl	through back loop
tog	together
tr	treble crochet
WS	wrong side
yfwd	yarn forward